Praise for Barbara Wren

'I first took my children to see Barbara Wren 15 years ago, and her principles and practices remain at the heart of my family life and my clinical practice as a doctor of medicine. She is a true inspiration for all who are interested in the art and science of being healthy. A superb author.'
Dr Stephen Hopwood MB CHB GMC Lic Ac

'Sharing the benefits of her experience, Wren provides the tools to restore our balance and become the shining beings that we really are.'
Nexus magazine

'I love Barbara Wren's work. I have personally benefitted from putting her words into practice.'
David R. Hamilton PhD, author of How Your Mind Can Heal Your Body

'Barbara is an inspirational teacher. This book is a vital tool for manifesting our greatest potential, physical vitality and emotional and spiritual wellbeing.'
Laura Bull, homeopath and meditation teacher

'A fascinating and deeply thought-provoking book filled with information that will resonate with anyone interested in fulfilling their true potential.'
Andy Baggott, author of Blissology

'In the sea of books relating to health, Barbara Wren presents the mechanism of how the healthy human body functions, considers the main factors causing disease and provides techniques for restoring health and keeping the body in good condition. It is the foundation for achieving good health!'
Mariyanah Zlatareva, Publisher

OUR
RETURN
TO THE
LIGHT

By the same author:

Cellular Awakening (Hay House, 2009)

OUR
RETURN
TO THE
LIGHT

A New Path to Health and Healing

BARBARA WREN

HAY HOUSE

Carlsbad, California • New York City • London • Sydney
Johannesburg • Vancouver • Hong Kong • New Delhi

First published and distributed in the United Kingdom by:
Hay House UK Ltd, Astley House, 33 Notting Hill Gate, London W11 3JQ
Tel: +44 (0)20 3675 2450; Fax: +44 (0)20 3675 2451
www.hayhouse.co.uk

Published and distributed in the United States of America by:
Hay House Inc., PO Box 5100, Carlsbad, CA 92018-5100
Tel: (1) 760 431 7695 or (800) 654 5126
Fax: (1) 760 431 6948 or (800) 650 5115
www.hayhouse.com

Published and distributed in Australia by:
Hay House Australia Ltd, 18/36 Ralph St, Alexandria NSW 2015
Tel: (61) 2 9669 4299; Fax: (61) 2 9669 4144
www.hayhouse.com.au

Published and distributed in the Republic of South Africa by:
Hay House SA (Pty) Ltd, PO Box 990, Witkoppen 2068
Tel/Fax: (27) 11 467 8904
www.hayhouse.co.za

Published and distributed in India by:
Hay House Publishers India, Muskaan Complex, Plot No.3, B-2,
Vasant Kunj, New Delhi 110 070
Tel: (91) 11 4176 1620; Fax: (91) 11 4176 1630
www.hayhouse.co.in

Distributed in Canada by:
Raincoast, 9050 Shaughnessy St, Vancouver BC V6P 6E5
Tel: (1) 604 323 7100; Fax: (1) 604 323 2600

A catalogue record for this book is available from the British Library.

ISBN: 978-1-78180-071-3

Printed and bound in Great Britain by TJ International Ltd, Padstow, Cornwall

To my parents, Cissie and James Wren, my children and grandchildren, and to everyone who has awakened me on my journey.

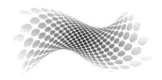

Contents

Introduction

Our Place in the Universe

Imagine a matrix of energy crisscrossing space-time around you, passing through you, connecting the Earth to the heavens above and beyond – an energetic matrix through which all things are connected. Picture your body on its journey through life, suffused with and surrounded by this energy. Picture your body as a vehicle – the vehicle that *you* are travelling in.

I'm fascinated by the question of how we can look after ourselves as we make our way through this world, unique and yet connected to the whole universe. How can we nourish ourselves? How can we nurture ourselves in every aspect of our life? How can we fully express who we are?

We come into this amazing world with all the equipment we need to be who we are. But to express ourselves fully, we need to maintain a clear connection to the universe. That means keeping our vehicle in top form both as a receiver and a transmitter of light. This is the means by which we are connected to the universal wisdom around us.

In my previous book, *Cellular Awakening*, I explained how the body held, stored and produced light, and the role of DNA in personalizing the light from the universe. DNA is effectively an expression of light, underpinning our nature as beings of light. When we're comfortable with ourselves and in our rightful position in the universe, and when we nourish ourselves correctly, our body will attract light and radiate the full expression of who we are.

Everything in our universe is energy, and every form of energy has a resonance. Each of us has a particular resonance. We also live under the influence of extraordinary energies and vibrations in conditions that are changing all the time. When we fit into our individual part of this jigsaw, we're able to express ourselves fully and have a sense of comfort, but when things become discordant and unresolved, we'll be out of touch with ourselves and feel discomfort. This discord can become disease. I approach disease as an expression of a discordant resonance that manifests when we're not being who we are.

How do we know who we are? To begin with, we already know that each of us is a particular expression of the universe. The moment in which we were conceived and the moment in which we were born were both heralded by very specific planetary blueprints in the heavens. Each of the planets has a different energy, a different quality of light and a different relationship with the metals and elements in our Earthly habitat. Mars, for example, has a particular relationship with copper, with the liver, with anger, with form, structure, flexibility and rigidity. All of the planets will affect our own individual make-up.

We also come into life with predispositions inherited from our ancestral lineage. The many generations that have gone before have left their trace. How they lived, what they thought, how their food was grown and prepared and whether they nurtured themselves and adhered to life's natural rules and laws will all have an impact on our body and its processes. None of us suddenly arrives here as a clean slate.

I'm fascinated by the predispositions that have shaped us into who we are now. The line that we've chosen to be born into at this time carries its own unique and wonderful story. We hold that story in the resonance of our body today. Our ancestral past is imprinted in and on our body, shaping its form and its potential to be a body of light.

Essentially it's light that connects us all. Light is ubiquitous. We're surrounded and suffused by it. Our body stores and produces it, expresses and transmits it. Light carries our sense of empathy. When we feel a resonance with a particular person, what is being transmitted between us is the light produced by our bodies.

Light connects us with others. It also connects the cells in our body. It's through light and colour that they communicate. Under ideal conditions, they allow the full spectrum of light to move through them. For this to happen, a cell needs to be healthy and clear. As soon as it becomes toxic, or not quite in harmony, it starts to refract, rather than channel, light, restricting the spectrum of colour transmitted and reducing the information that the light can carry. This will be reflected in the whole body.

The clearer we are, and the more light we're therefore able to produce, hold and transmit, the more we'll be able to receive and share the universal wisdom that's readily available to us all. The optimal way of being is contained in this wisdom.

We don't have to look very far to see how this is being distorted in the world today. The optimal human state is one of peace, harmony and connectedness, not of war, hatred and separateness. But look around you — what do you see?

It's very important to acknowledge the full scope of our connectedness. It reaches beyond our human connections to our connection with the Earth and our recognition of how much life depends upon her. It also extends to our connection to the upper energies, the heavens.

If we acknowledge these connections and are in harmony with them, reflecting and transmitting the full spectrum of light, it's impossible for there to be stress in our life. If we could all live like this, what a world it would be. How can we make this happen?

We know that we're primarily comprised of water. Water is the medium that holds messages. In Eastern philosophy, the Water element is where we store fear. A very simple principle is at work here: as soon as we're stressed, we start to become dehydrated. The resonance of stress diminishes the body's hydration, increases the level of fear and, as the Water element is linked to the central nervous system, initiates dysfunction there, too. Stress causes a contraction of the fluids of the body, which in turn contracts the wisdom we can hold, diminishing our capacity to have a clear picture of who we are. Throughout this book we'll be looking at how stress affects the body to the core of its being and what we can do about it.

Changes in planetary charge and the availability of light also have a profound influence on the body's processes and connectedness. Once every two hours, the charge of each of the planets changes slightly, altering its vibration and resonance. Each change in resonance affects a different set of organs in the body. So, as we go through a 24-hour day, we have 12 influences, at two-hour intervals, reminding us to bring a particular set of organs and emotions into balance. Alongside this planetary rhythm, the sun and moon play out their cycles of day and night, light and dark, which also affect the body. Through these rhythms underscoring the passage of time, the universe has an in-built system that keeps our body in a dynamic flow.

The lunar influence, with its monthly transition from new to full and its tidal impulse of drawing up and letting go, is similarly profound. Full and new moons create very different conditions. At the full moon, the increased number of positive ions in the air tends to create discomfort. For most people, the new moon is a much more comfortable time, as then we're bathed in negative ions. The monthly cycle of the moon also gives us the opportunity to pull our body back into balance.

In addition to these cycles, seasonal changes bring their own rhythm. Traditional Chinese Medicine (TCM) identifies five seasons, each with an associated emotion. The seasons offer another brush to sweep us back into balance. Whether or not we choose to take the opportunity, we're all affected by the seasonal changes as the year moves around. Here we are, between heaven and Earth, connected to all things.

Having an awareness of our body and its processes, and paying attention to the effect of cosmic rhythms and cycles on it, will enable us to maintain it in the best possible shape and state of health, while responding fluidly to the external influences on our internal being.

Also, our body has a memory that records as much as our mind. The imprint of events, particularly physical shock and trauma, can become lodged in the body or have a recurrent effect – often on an annual basis. It's very important that we accept, stay with and work through these somatic memories, otherwise they can disrupt our energetic blueprint. I've worked with people in my healing practice who've overcome an addiction, for example, but still suffer from its physical effects because no work has been done to help their body move back into balance. I've known people who've overcome heroin addiction through working with the mind, and years later, because the physical body hasn't reconfigured the new mental blueprint, have been unable to have a baby. The energetic blueprint that would have enabled conception to occur just wasn't in place.

When helping the body create a new energetic blueprint after shock, trauma and stress, it's vital to recognize the connection between the body and Mother Earth. The Earth's composition actually provides a template for the energetic blueprint. That's why we call the planet Mother Earth: she is the provider and nurturer of life.

When our energetic blueprint is clear and unimpaired, life follows in a spontaneous, connected way from within – from the light we're holding. Our body becomes a microcosm of the macrocosm. In *Cellular Awakening*, I explored the idea that each cell is a microcosm of the macrocosm, and I want to take that further here.

I call the cell membrane the cell's 'doorman', because it determines whether the macrocosm, in the form of light, can pass through into the microcosm of the cell so that it becomes our being. Once it's in there, we can't help but be who we are. That's when things really start to flow spontaneously; when we find our path and begin to reach our full potential. Surely that's what life is all about?

So, the condition of the cell's membrane is of great importance. It affects how much information from the macrocosm is able to get through to us. The more we look after our body, the more information about ourselves and our purpose comes through.

The condition of the body, including hydration, pH, temperature, light availability, retention, storage and production and how oxygen is drawn in for respiration, is crucial to the quality of this connection. In addition, flow — movement — is fundamentally important. I see healing as the creation of freedom and movement on all levels of our being. As, for example, the body becomes more fluid and starts to open up, revelations about its inherited predispositions start to appear and those predispositions can be released. It's so important that we're able to feel freedom and movement and adapt to life's ever-changing conditions.

Stress, in any form, will inhibit freedom and movement. As it becomes entrenched, the body itself will become increasingly rigid, losing its ability to flow, adapt and find comfort in exploring.

At the present time, stress and fear are beginning to paralyse so many of us. We run the risk of becoming imprisoned by our own fear and by the fear emanating around us. When a lot of people are afraid, fear becomes a very powerful collective expression. This can distract us from our intended path, obscuring who we really are. It directly impacts our body and can lead to a disconnection from consciousness and conscience, which are fundamental to personal integrity. We can see this happening in the world around us.

We also see people who are weighed down by heavy predispositions that have come down from previous generations. At the level of society, these appear in the dominant vision of sickness and disease and in the way agriculture and education are conducted. Currently, this is coming to a head: our society's sickness is becoming more and more visible. However, if we can see it, we can change it.

In the following pages we'll look at the predispositions that have led us to the vulnerable position in which we seem to be collectively. But we'll also explore the opportunity for rectification that is now being offered to us. We're living in a time of maximum photon activity, and I believe we can draw on the vast amount of light that is now available to us and utilize it to transform the conditions around us.

I see our place in the universe very clearly: we are beings who manifest the incorporation of heaven and Earth. We all share this position; however, because each of us is unique, each with an individual history and make-up, we each represent a different part of the overall puzzle. For me, the most exciting thing about the journey of life on Earth is discovering how we fit into that puzzle. In order to do this we have to be able to receive universal wisdom, so it all starts with sensing ourselves as a resonance, hearing the music of that resonance and finding the harmony that will guide us to our very own place in the universe. Then we can work as part of the collective to remove the predispositions which, I feel, have ultimately led to the sort of world we're living in today.

If we can dance harmoniously, as who we are, to the universal rhythms, flowing, happy and free of fear, this will be a wonderful world – and that, I believe, should be our intention. In this book we'll look at the opportunity we have, as a result of the changing resonance of the Earth and the cosmos, to make this happen. We'll also examine how we can store and produce light and transmit it to each other most effectively. We are a resonance coming from and returning to light, and it's our lifetime's work to manifest the light we carry within us and radiate it out into the greater cosmos.

Let's set the scene within our body, our vehicle through life.

PART I

OUR BODY
OF LIGHT

Chapter 1

A Manifestation of Light

We are a resonance, a manifestation of light – slowed-down light creating matter. But we have a physical form, too, in which energy and matter come together between heaven and Earth, above and below.

I believe that in this form our true potential for health lies in the cells of the body; they are the microcosm that controls the macrocosm. So, if we want to get a picture of our health at any moment in time and change it for the better, we need to be able to understand and affect it at a cellular level. Accordingly, let's draw a thumbnail sketch of how the perfect cell in the body should function.

THE PERFECT CELL

Each cell in the body has a membrane that is made up of three layers and holds a charge. Overnight the body cleanses itself following the metabolic processes of the day, and upon waking, the nucleus of the cell should be positive, the inside of the cell membrane should be negative and the outer cell membrane should be positive: positive–negative–positive. The differential between the outside of the cell membrane and the inside is hugely important, and if we were able to measure that differential, it would be the perfect way of measuring the resonance of that cell.

Within the inner layer of the cell membrane are the calcium gates, which allow things in and out. Our life depends on being able to integrate different energies into our cells – for example, nutrients from the soil and light and oxygen from the air and sun. So, in order to attract the maximum donation of electrons from the world around us, the perfect situation is to have a very strong positive charge on the outer cell membrane; this way we can attract the maximum number of negatively charged subatomic particles: the electrons. Then photon energy becomes trapped in 'electron clouds' around each cell and attracts oxygen.

The cells are surrounded by extracellular fluids, or humours, inhabited by tiny particles or microzymas, which influence the state of the cell. The 19th-century French chemist and biologist Antoine Béchamp identified 16 stages or states that these microzyma could exhibit and, more importantly, discovered that they could move backward and forward through these stages and create many different influences intended to serve the body.

The important thing here is that we're taught, wrongly, to believe that disease comes from the outside; in Béchamp's model, if we control the quality of our extracellular fluids, we control the 16 stages of the microzymas and our vulnerability to disease. According to Béchamp, all disease is created from within.

In the perfect situation, the cell will make its energy (adenosine triphosphate or ATP) from 80 per cent oxygen and 20 per cent glucose, and in the worst-case scenario it will make it from 20 per cent oxygen and 80 per cent glucose. There are many stages in between. The trouble is that when the cell no longer functions optimally, the cell membrane potential weakens over time in a diminishing cycle in which it can't attract the maximum number of photons so it can't trap sufficient oxygen, and the less oxygen that is attracted, the more the cell has to rely on glucose to create its energy.

There is also a daily exchange of electrolytes in the cell. During the day, calcium and sodium move into the cell through the calcium gates and push out their opposites: calcium pushes out magnesium and sodium pushes out potassium. At night the process is reversed, because the charge of the Earth changes and we are affected by the moon, which draws out the sodium and calcium and allows the magnesium and potassium to return.

We know that there are not enough calcium gates for this electrolyte exchange to be an entirely physical one. Although this is not what we're taught, I believe that the majority of this exchange must be via transmutation, where one substance simply changes into another, and the amount of oxygen and number of photons present have an enormous influence on this process – in fact, they provide the energy for it to take place.

So, what causes the cell to stop operating in this perfect state? The simple answer is dehydration. When we become dehydrated, the body works to protect our remaining water levels by coating the cell membrane in cholesterol. But as soon as that happens, it influences the day/night exchange and changes the charge of the cell. The result of this defence mechanism is that transmutation is affected and sodium and calcium start to be left in the cell. This weakens and hardens the cell membrane, which then registers a drop in resonance. The change of charge also means that the cell's ability to attract electrons and photons is reduced. If this situation is not reversed, the cell gradually drops out of the bigger information picture – out of the perfect rhythm and resonance of the body. This is a process that can lead to encapsulation and isolation, and it marks the beginning of dis-ease.

What Causes Dehydration?

In Traditional Chinese Medicine, the Water element holds fear and anxiety, and winter is the time of the bladder and kidneys. So any kind of stress – nutritional, lifestyle, ancestral or emotional – will have a physical manifestation: it will cause dehydration.

Eastern medicine teaches that if this situation continues for two years, then the body goes into dehydration alert, creating a build-up of cholesterol within the cell membrane that is sufficient to protect the cell from dehydrating to death. It's easy to see that in this scenario the cell membrane is compromised, due to the hardening process, and when there is this depth of dehydration, we are vulnerable to disease at a deep level, too. So, our job is to reassure the body that it is not dehydrated. This is done by sending a message from the colon, which is the organ that registers dehydration. We will look at this in more detail later.

FATS AND OILS

Over the last two years it has become obvious to me that one of the biggest causes of stress on the body, and therefore of dehydration, is our intake of fats and oils, particularly heated fats.

The problem is that most people, in my experience, can't break down fats and oils. Ideally, the liver breaks down fats and oils and controls hydration, while the kidneys act as filters. If we consume too many fats and oils, however, the liver can't break them down, so they go through the lacteals in the villi in the small intestine straight into the lymph, slowing it down and creating stagnation and congestion. This is a source of stress and therefore dehydration.

The lymph drips into the blood with each heartbeat: the left feed-in carries the lymph from the whole of the body, including the left ear, and usually manifests the largest stagnation problem, and the right carries the lymph from the rest of the head. Slow movement of the lymph will ultimately cause the red blood cells to clump, which in turn will affect the oxygenation and the lining of the blood cells, impairing the escape of glucose into the cells to help make ATP. So it's very easy to see why there is so much heart disease around today.

But all disease starts with stress, which will cause dehydration, affect movement throughout the body and lead to stagnation and the build-up of toxins. When toxicity reaches this point, particularly in young children, the body throws up inflammation, in the form of perhaps a sore throat or an ear infection, to resolve the situation. However, if we continue to press the body in this way, it ceases to be able to create localized inflammations like these and instead the cells affected start to drop out of communication with the rest of the body.

What is clear to me is that it is only when hydration is operating well that the lymph can operate, the body can cleanse itself and the immune system can remain strong. So, the first thing to become aware of is the number of heated fats in our diet – biscuits, cake, pastries, etc. – and keep these to an absolute minimum, if we eat them at all. Saturated fats – butter, coconut oil, and animal fats – are safer to heat because they don't have double-carbon bonds; however, I'd suggest it is wise to avoid eating heated fats and oils as much as possible to avoid overtaxing the liver, the organ of hydration.

It's also important to consider the percentage of calories of fats and oils in our diet overall. For example, many people consider nuts and seeds to be healthy and so eat large numbers of them, but these are concentrated foods that can also create stress and dehydration.

So, one of the biggest influences on the body's overall health is fats and oils, because if we're challenging our liver, we will stay dehydrated. This is the reason why so many of us are suffering from allergies nowadays. It isn't possible to have an allergic response unless you're very dehydrated. What is happening here is that the colon registers the dehydration, and the mast cells respond by releasing histamines; the more dehydrated the body, the more histamines are produced.

Some oils, of course, are required for the maintenance of health, especially the essential fatty acids, but we can only make use of them if the liver isn't overloaded with heated fats and surplus oils. In my experience, once you restore liver function by not eating masses of fats and oils, then the necessary fats and oils can get through to where they're needed. This is particularly true in conditions where DHA is important, such as MS. And once hydration levels are lifted, healing can start from within.

The key thing to remember is that the body is very resourceful and doesn't need high quantities of anything – even good fats and oils.

SODIUM AND CALCIUM

The most difficult things to change are those that are calcified, and, as we have just seen, when transmutation is affected by the body being dehydrated, calcium and its travelling partner sodium are displaced and left inside the cell, creating a hardening picture and a drop in resonance of that cell. How can we remedy this situation?

First of all, it's important to think about the water we drink. Tap water can contain large amounts of inorganic calcium, which seeps into the supply as it rises through the layers of chalk.

We also need good supplies of silica to maintain the flexibility of our cells and keep everything in place by ejecting what isn't required. Food sources of silica include nettles, horsetail and the stems of plants like wheatgrass and barleygrass.

THE PH BALANCE

The pH of the body is also important, particularly of the extracellular fluids, because stagnation there will affect the microzymas and therefore the state of the whole cell.

We are alkaline beings, but all of the body's metabolic processes produce acidity, so we have to work quite hard to remain alkaline. The blood has to maintain a pH level of 7.34 otherwise the body would die, so that remains alkaline, but often at a cost to the rest of the body: joints start to change, muscles ache, blood sugar dips and spikes, and the mind is not always clear.

From a nutritional perspective, if we want to maintain an alkaline state in the body, vegetables are our best friends, particularly if they're grown biodynamically. The reason I say this is because we want to minimize the stress our food has on our body, and food grown in harmony with the people who eat it has a connection with them and a similarity of energy. Maybe this is part of the reason why macrobiotic diets are effective for some people, because they are tuned to work with the harmony of the body.

FULL-SPECTRUM LIGHT

Finally, the cell's ability to trap photons of light is vital in ensuring that the maximum quota of oxygen is attracted to maintain that perfect picture of ATP being made from 80 per cent oxygen and 20 per cent glucose.

What we now know is that the body not only traps and stores light but also produces light. Each cell produces measurable light in the form of 'bio-photons' from within its DNA helix. The 'shedding' of bio-photons has been photographed, and it has been noted that there is a huge increase in the shedding when one person is healing another.

Communication via light is seen most clearly in the body at a cellular level. If the resonance of the cells is high, their membranes are soft and the full spectrum of light is hitting all of them, then full communication will take place. But if a cell is in a lowered resonance or diseased, then it will refract the light and that will be passed on, so there will be a diminution of the colours – and the information – available to the rest of the cells.

This is why I am passionate about old-fashioned nursing and techniques that carry the full spectrum of light, such as castor oil packing to help regenerate liver function; Epsom salts baths, which act as a natural tranquillizer for the body; and methods that support routes of elimination that reduce the body's stress level and help it to rehydrate. I've included all these techniques in the Appendix, but in the meantime I hope you are now able to envisage each cell in your body as a microcosm and to understand its importance in bringing in and utilizing elements from the macrocosm. How the two interact plays a vital role in our health – and our connection to universal wisdom.

Chapter 2

Preconception, Pregnancy and Birth

Let's start now by looking at the very beginning of life. When thinking about fertility, the most important thing to consider is light. Is there enough light within the body to support the creation of new life?

Think of your body as a test tube. See the conditions in that test tube as the determining factor in relation to the outcome of the experiment. In this case, though, it's not an experiment, it's fertility and conception.

PRECONCEPTION

First of all, we need to examine what's happening in the cells of the body. Remember that the important thing is to allow the maximum amount of light — the macrocosm — to get inside the cells — our microcosm.

The electrical charge of the cell is crucial here. We need the nucleus to have a strong positive charge, the inside of the cell membrane to have a strong negative charge and the outside of the cell membrane to have a strong positive charge. Then negatively charged subatomic particles will migrate and create a cloud of electrons around each cell. Photons of light will become entrapped in these electron clouds and be drawn into the cell. The clouds need to be held around the cell membrane, because if they float off, the messages delivered via the photons will not enter the cell.

The overall charge of the cell changes depending on where it is in the 24-hour cycle and the health of the body. It takes a full 24-hour cycle to return a cell to its correct charge in a healthy individual.

Electrons are donated to us by Mother Earth from the ground, through our feet, and through the food we eat. Essential fatty acids, omega 3 and omega 6, have the potential to create a lot of electron clouds. So, in order to create the correct conditions for fertility, we need to be working on the nutritional requirements within the cell, as well as looking after our general health.

This means maximizing hydration. The body probably never needs to be more perfectly hydrated than when it's supporting the beginning of new life. So, the mother and father need to take in adequate fluids to prepare for conception.

Something else to consider when addressing fertility is how well the liver is functioning. In Traditional Chinese Medicine, one of the roles of the liver is to plan the body's functions. So it will determine whether or not, and when, ovulation takes place, when conception occurs and when the baby is born.

As well as these factors, an individual's predispositions will also impact their fertility. So, preconception care has to include exploring, as far as possible, what's gone on in previous generations in order to see what kinds of trends have carried through.

The human body adapts to its environment and circumstances. It will never work against itself, even in extreme conditions, for example during a famine. Whatever the situation, it does its best to adapt. Of course, this means that certain life-preserving changes have to take place. These will be imprinted on the energetic blueprint of the next generation as stress.

Unresolved emotional trauma can have the same impact. Unresolved grief can be inherited as a resonance of stress.

These memory traces are what homoeopathy refers to as 'miasms' and TCM five element theory as 'causative factors'. Whatever the name, the stress will dehydrate the cells and so their capacity to hold light and information will be diminished. The exchange of sodium and calcium and potassium and magnesium will be incomplete, and the charge of the membranes will be weakened. This will impact directly on the cells' ability to accept photons of light.

Therefore, it's useful to know if there have been nutritional issues in previous generations, particularly in terms of famine or deprivation. If there have, conditions need to be rectified to ensure optimal electron uptake from the diet and therefore optimal light within the body. This is true in any event, not only when preparing for conception.

Something else to consider is the body's pH. When we rise each morning, at the end of the test tube's 24-hour cycle, we should feel completely refreshed and cleansed, and the pH of our body should be alkaline. If the body does slip into dehydration or acidity, the charge of the tissues will change, the day/night electrolyte exchange will be affected, the body's resonance with all the universal rhythms will change and it may not be able to support fertility at all.

Overall, when it comes to fertility, we have to take into account everything that might influence the charge of the mother's and the father's body, so that the imprint on both the egg and the sperm is as good as it can possibly be. It's vital to consider what has happened in a person's own history, and also their parents' history, particularly dietary history, and whether the reproductive areas are clear, with the freedom and movement necessary to bring new life into the world.

We're seeing so many problems around fertility nowadays, particularly as a result of the number of girls who are using the contraceptive pill during puberty. Zinc, for example, is vitally important in relation to fertility; and the contraceptive pill eliminates it from the body.

Also, during puberty the body has to work incredibly hard; it's a very demanding phase. Looking at a woman's case history at that time can reveal a lot. I'm coming across so many cases of unduly heavy and painful periods, both during puberty and beyond, which indicate that the liver is out of balance; if a woman's liver isn't doing its job properly, her body will utilize the large mucosal area in the uterus to effect elimination (fibroids are often referred to as 'secondary livers'). But the liver is the body's main route for elimination; the reproductive system shouldn't be called on as back-up.

We're also seeing an awful lot of cases of polycystic ovaries, as well as cases in which the whole of the endocrine system is really struggling – with that struggle going on throughout puberty. Quite often thyroid functioning is significant in this. Endometriosis is also becoming increasingly common. The whole reproductive picture has become very challenging for women.

If we improve the conditions in the test tube, however, we can improve the cellular function and maximize the amount of light, which is crucial not only for conception but for everything to do with fertility. Preparation is so important; preconceptual care can optimize everything.

PREGNANCY

Pregnancy tends to be a very challenging time for women in the West, as many of them have to balance it with the demands of work and nurturing other children, and, unless in very good health and very strong mentally, they also have to endure a lot of interference in both the pregnancy and the birth.

If the body is out of balance to begin with, ovulation may not take place, or, if fertilization does occur, it may take place in the Fallopian tube, and the embryo may become lodged there rather than in the uterus – an ectopic pregnancy. In this case the charge of the body is far enough out to lead to a potentially dangerous situation. Likewise, in cases of *placenta praevia*, where the placenta attaches itself over the birth canal, the body's imbalance becomes potentially life-threatening. In these cases the baby has to be delivered by Caesarean section, as otherwise the placenta will be born first, leaving the baby deprived. This is the result of the uterine cells' charge not being strong enough to attract the placenta into the correct position.

Similarly, breech presentation, which also presents problems in birthing, highlights the incorrect orientation of the baby, or the placenta, in the uterus, as do situations in which the cord becomes wrapped around the baby's neck. Here the baby has not been able to move freely, so the placenta is not in a high enough position on the uterine wall.

It's interesting to note how many babies are now presenting posteriorly. The fact that they're the wrong way around means that labour will take longer, as the baby reconfigures its position. One has to wonder how much electromagnetic interference could be contributing to these situations, given the number of women who are working all day with computers and phones.

Diet may also be a factor. Later in the book we'll look at how our diets have changed over the years and the effect this has had. Briefly, however, modern diets include heated fats of all types – saturated, non-saturated and poly-unsaturated – and, as already mentioned, the liver struggles to metabolize them. Also, if it's being deluged with fats, it is unable to utilize the important omega oils, including omega 3 and particularly EPA, which can help the endocrine system, and DHA, which is needed by the central nervous system. These are incredibly important in the preparation for having a baby. What the mother and father eat during preconception, coupled with what the mother eats throughout her pregnancy, contributes to the baby being fully nourished.

One of the easiest ways to approach diet is to remember that the body is predominantly made up of water. The diet also needs to be adjusted in relation to a person's predispositions and shouldn't present a challenge to their system. Wheat can present particular challenges because of the way it's cultivated and the way bread is made. It's a harsh grain and less easily digested than the gentler grains. Dairy produce, often targeted at expectant mothers, also presents the body with challenges. Given how cattle are reared and nourished, and the treatments milk products undergo, it's not surprising.

It's important to go through the diet very carefully in order to identify areas that might present issues, in particular how much fat, especially heated fat, is present and whether the liver can deal with it. What I tend to find is that if the liver is struggling, the ability of the body to absorb food as a whole will be affected. Keeping heated fats to an absolute minimum can also play a huge part in preventing feelings of sickness during pregnancy.

It's also important that your diet resonates with you personally. Blessing food before eating it brings about a merging of your energy and the energy of the food you are about to eat, creating a resonance between the food and you. Eating local food and being involved in its preparation will help increase that resonance, as will the state of your own energy.

Eating is not just about vitamins and minerals, however, but also about the vitality being taken in. So, diet should also be about drawing in an optimal amount of strong electron energy from Mother Earth.

Looking after the body properly will ensure that everything is lined up correctly, the charge is right and everything is in the right position for birth.

BIRTH

If the uterus holds the correct charge, the baby is in the correct position, the liver — the planner — is happy, the muscular flexibility of the uterus is good and the cervix soft, then birth can proceed very well.

The cervix needs to be softened through massage with almond oil during the last few weeks of the pregnancy. The muscular flexibility and softness of the cervix are also very much dependent on the four electrolytes. Sodium and calcium aid contraction, while potassium and magnesium aid relaxation. In the Western world there tends to be a lot of sodium and calcium in our diet and a deficiency of potassium and magnesium.

I often come across people who have an issue with magnesium. It has a lot to do with placing the calcium in the correct position. This is very important, particularly in terms of a cell's ability to clear itself and have the correct charge so that the baby is in the perfect position. In cases where there are issues, I tend to use magnesium during labour to help relaxation. Essentially, though, it should all be in the preparation.

When it comes to the actual birth, ideally the woman will be able to go to a place of privacy. It's a terrible pity if she can't be totally in touch with her baby during birth because she is distracted by what's going on around her. We certainly don't want adrenaline being triggered in the mother – this is not at all helpful for the baby. Unfortunately, though, this is the norm in the Western world; we've moved a long way from how it should be. Women also naturally want gravity to help in the process rather than to find themselves lying on their backs with monitors all over them. In this position, not only is gravity unable to fulfil its role, but the pelvis is unable to move in more than one direction.

Ideally, after careful and thorough preparation, the baby will be gently expelled by the natural process of the uterus – not be pushed out with great violence, with the mother pushing like mad, not breathing and cutting off her and the baby's oxygen supply.

If the whole process has been carefully controlled by the baby and the mother working together, the cervix has been well massaged and the muscles are working well, there is no reason for any tearing.

After the birth, the baby should be placed on the mother's belly, skin to skin, so that it moves to find the nipple and starts to suckle. Breastfeeding should be a pleasant experience. It's good practice to massage the nipple area during the last three months of pregnancy with the mother's own urine, so the nipples are tougher than usual and don't become sore and uncomfortable when breastfeeding takes place.

Soon after the baby's birth, the placenta will be delivered. We're the only mammal on the planet that doesn't eat the placenta, and we really should. Rather than being discarded as waste, it should be treasured, dehydrated and prepared for consumption. I encourage expectant mothers to put a piece of raw placenta in a smoothie to consume straightaway and then make sure they have some dried placenta to take over a period of time. This will help both mother and baby as their relationship develops, as well as helping to rebalance the mother's body.

Chapter 3

From Infancy to Puberty and Beyond

In coming back to the light, we need to understand the stress load we're holding in the body, our vehicle. This is the accumulation of stress from inheritance, gestation, birth and our life so far. Even if food and lifestyle during this time don't create actual illnesses or issues, they are often challenging, so they create stress, and it's the build-up of stress that holds us back from fulfilling our potential in adulthood.

EARLY TRANSITIONS

Three transitions between birth and the age of two are vital. When these transitions don't go smoothly, it can mark the beginning of illnesses that can build up during the formative years and manifest in more serious issues in adulthood.

1. Copper–Zinc Rebalancing

As a pregnancy draws towards its close, the level of copper in the mother's body starts to increase, due to copper's role in triggering the contractions that enable the baby to be gently delivered. An increase in the level of copper will lead to a decrease in the level of zinc. The copper/zinc ratio is very important, as a preponderance of copper underlies co-dependency.

When a baby is inside the mother, it is of course totally dependent on her for survival. Being born is its first step towards independence. Though by no means independent at this stage, the baby needs an input of zinc to help it rebalance after the physical separation of birth. By eating her placenta, the mother will boost the level of zinc in her colostrum. It's very important that the baby receives this zinc-rich food.

We'll start to see exactly how important when we look at puberty, but whenever I come across a co-dependent, addictive nature, I know that copper has had too great an influence over that person.

2. The Sodium–Potassium Switch

The second transition involves the minerals sodium and potassium. Prior to birth, sodium levels in the foetus are higher than those of potassium. During infancy, this needs to switch, so that potassium becomes dominant over sodium.

When weaning starts, the mother will be introducing the baby to the vegetable kingdom and all its beautiful, electron-abundant, potassium-rich foods. She also should be doing it through her own diet while she's feeding the baby.

It's very important that levels of sodium don't remain too high in the diet of mother and infant, as sodium, and its partner, calcium, initiate contraction in the body. Since sodium and calcium always co-exist, a high level of sodium will also mean a high level of calcium. Rather than baby's test tube having a predominance of contraction-inducing minerals, a more ideal environment would be to have a predominance of the relaxing minerals, potassium and magnesium. Unfortunately, these tend to be depleted in the soils we grow our food in these days, and there is a shortage of vegetables in our diet.

3. The Porous Small Intestine

Until the age of two, an infant's small intestine remains porous. The diets of both mother and child need to take this into account.

The small intestine's porosity allows the protein molecules in gluten and dairy products to pass through its walls (often called leaky gut syndrome). To avoid this, it's advisable that gluten and dairy are left out of the diet in favour of softer grains, including millet, rice, quinoa and amaranth. It's also important to avoid using heated fats as far as possible.

Essential fatty acids and phospholipids are necessary to help the central nervous system and to seal the small intestine.

4. The Blood–Brain Barrier

Another vital formation that should take place during infancy is the blood–brain barrier. This protects the brain from foreign, toxic matter. Its formation depends on adequate amounts of iodine, the DHA component of omega 3, vitamin D3 (made within the body from sunlight) and zinc. These ingredients are vital throughout life.

Vitamin D3 is actually one of the most important nutrients, as this light from the cosmos brings an amazing resonance of how things are and how they should be. Therefore, we need to be able to receive it in a completely untransformed or undamaged way – and this is only possible when the body is healthy at the cellular level.

If the blood–brain barrier isn't operating properly, then it's a freeway to the brain, not only for protein molecules but also for heavy metals (for example, lead and mercury), pesticides, etc. So the blood–brain barrier is very much the first cousin to the small intestine, as it protects the higher aspects of the person at the brain level.

It also follows that if toxins are crossing the blood–brain barrier and poisoning the brain, this will result in a change of behaviour.

VACCINATIONS

Earlier I mentioned the value of a diet that has a gentle resonance with us in avoiding the stress that will lead to dehydration. We need to do as much as we can to avoid introducing harmful stresses to our body. Many people are concerned about the invasive testing that takes place as a matter of routine during pregnancy, including ultrasounds. Vaccines constitute another potential stress-loading for the body, and there are now so many of them. It seems totally abnormal that 35 vaccines can be given before a child has even started school.

The aim of exploring family history during preconception care is to identify appropriate methods for strengthening the immune system. Plenty of literature nowadays highlights how our diet has changed and the adverse impact this has had on the immune system. The book *Left in the Dark* by Graham Gynn and Tony Wright illustrates this very clearly. Vaccines allegedly create greater immunity, but I'd suggest people do very extensive homework before even considering getting their newly born and young children vaccinated.

If we have a perfectly balanced baby and it's given a series of multiple vaccines, there is no doubt it will become stressed. This will lead to a degree of dehydration, which will be felt in the colon. This may show up in a number of ways or may be difficult to detect. The baby may become a bit constipated or may not appear as serene as usual. For a baby who already has a degree of dehydration, the extra stress of multiple vaccines can lead to skin issues, including eczema. For a baby whose predispositions are already manifest at skin level, the added stress of vaccination will create deeper issues. The stress will increase the degree of dehydration, and symptoms may start to manifest in the lungs – possibly asthma or a vulnerability towards colds. The big thing to remember about the lungs is that they are the seat of depression. It is such a tragedy, at the beginning of life, to push a child towards a lack of joy and a predisposition for depression.

If a child with a predisposition that hasn't yet manifested in the lungs is given the added stress of vaccination, this can lead to the predisposition being manifested in the central nervous system. In these cases, autism, night terrors, agitation and other personality changes may appear.

I remember the first autistic child I worked with. Before he'd been vaccinated, his parents had been asked if there was any asthma in the family. His father had been adopted, so they weren't actually sure. It is always beneficial to find out the family history if at all possible.

The assessment of energy and hydration levels in a baby or young child is a very subtle process, but all the relevant information is there if we look very carefully at the family history to see what may come in if the infant is subjected to stress. This seems to me to be a good way of considering the pros and cons of vaccination.

I believe that vaccination creates unnecessary stress on a child's body, but whether to vaccinate or not is entirely a personal decision. If you want to understand more about the subject, I would recommend reading Trevor Gunn's enlightening work.

CHILDHOOD

When looking at a child's early health, it is possible to assess the sum total of stress experienced during the transition from babyhood. As we know already, stress creates dehydration, which in turn makes the lymph movement sluggish and the blood likely to clump. If the body cannot cleanse itself adequately, then the pH in the test tube changes and the body starts to become inflamed. We tend to see inflammation as a dangerous, as opposed to transitional, process; but it is a natural rebalancing that involves heat, and so has the ability to resolve the situation. Fever or temperature is the body's way of resolving something, and its ultimate purpose is to cleanse the body. Cleansing occurs naturally when the body heats up, as the blood moves more quickly then and the lymph becomes thinner. Hence it is not unusual for children to have fevers during teething, and common complaints among infants are sore throats, temperatures and swollen lymph nodes. These are all signs of congestion and lack of cleansing working to resolve themselves.

This is particularly evident if you look at a child whose lifestyle and diet are unsuitable by the age of two. In such cases, the cleansing process may have become so impaired that the child starts to produce regular fevers.

Childhood illnesses are of great significance because they show which area of the body is struggling. They also give a very good indication of the overall stresses that have been inherited and are affecting the child and influencing the body's ability to cleanse.

The lack of ability to cleanse will ultimately lead to toxicity in later life. What I mean by 'toxicity' is that the charge of the cell and the cell membrane will change, so the ability to hold big electron clouds to attract oxygen and photons will be negatively affected. To put it simply, the larger the electron clouds, the more light a person carries and radiates.

Sleep

To understand the full picture of a child's life, an important aspect to consider is sleeping patterns from birth to pre-pubescence.

If night terrors are present, it is helpful to give an Epsom salts bath before bed. Epsom salts are extremely detoxing because they are composed of magnesium sulphate. In certain conditions, particularly in cases of children with autism spectrum disorders, the sulphur taken in through food isn't converted into sulphate in the body, which is a necessary process to help the detoxification of the cells. As Epsom salts introduce the sulphate form, they can have a profound effect on helping the child release any heavy metals.

However, among most children aged five or older, night terrors are rare, and poor sleeping patterns are more commonly due to blood sugar, with the child unable to maintain stable blood sugar levels throughout the night. A hungry child won't sleep, and that's biochemical. Remember that low blood sugar can be described as the inability to hold calcium levels correctly in the blood, and this relates back to our day/night electrolyte exchange. However, this issue can be resolved using diet, in particular making sure that the child eats a snack before bed, and looking at magnesium intake.

Skin Issues

Skin issues, in particular eczema, are a common complaint in childhood. To discover their cause, it is important to look at the child's colon and digestive health and ask why the child is becoming over-heated and why there is a lack of soothing.

To answer these questions, it's important to understand that the movement and positioning of calcium and magnesium are vital for soothing the skin and keeping it healthy. We also know that zinc is required for skin integrity, which again highlights the importance of the copper–zinc transition in infancy.

The conventional treatment for eczema is steroid creams, which work by suppressing the symptoms. However, if skin issues are suppressed, then there is a risk that they will go deeper, to the lungs, and create some level of depression in the child, as the lungs are the intake-of-*chi* area and the seat of depression. An illness affecting the lungs (a vital organ) is potentially more dangerous than one affecting the skin (a lesser organ) and, in my experience, when a child's eczema is suppressed, it is often replaced by asthma, which can again affect the child's potential.

Throat Issues

Many children are plagued with coughs and colds throughout childhood, and these are usually blamed on the latest bug or virus doing the rounds. However, it is my experience that the predisposition to throat issues is due to a lack of cleansing. The body's manner of resolving this issue is to heat itself up by creating a fever, which warms and thins the lymph, enabling it to clear and move.

Recurrent throat issues, however, are a sure sign that there is something in the child's diet or lifestyle that is over-challenging and over-stressing the body. As a consequence, a recurrent throat issue should raise the alarm. If we let the illness run its course but don't deal with the source of inflammation (usually diet), the body will have to resolve the situation again and again. However, suppressing these eruptions with prescription medicines (e.g. antibiotics or antivirals) is even more suppressive, because then the resolution can't take place and trouble will just be stored up for a later date. Old naturopaths used to say that you can only suppress an acute manifestation three times, because after the third suppression it will go deeper. So, if we start to suppress these throat issues, we'll push them into the lungs. Suppressing an issue so that it moves from one level to another is the worst possible thing we can do.

Resolving the issue is simple: we need to create movement by introducing more fluids and ensuring that the child is following an unchallenging diet.

Ear Infections

In the five elements system in Traditional Chinese Medicine, there is a connection between the ears and the kidneys – the ears are the orifice of the kidneys; they are the same shape, and both are governed by the Water element. So ear infections usually indicate dehydration and lack of movement of fluids, and therefore incomplete cleansing. This is particularly true in childhood, because then the ear canals are quite small and easily blocked, which, especially when combined with an excess of toxins to eliminate, means they are highly susceptible to recurrent problems.

It is interesting to note that dehydration and inflammation of the ear mucosa also indicate that the child's copper–zinc levels are unbalanced, and so the child's parents might also notice behavioural issues. For example, the child might be slightly awkward, or not particularly compliant at school. If the body is struggling, it doesn't tend to show up just in a physical manifestation, but through all the levels of being. Therefore, it is also useful to look at behaviour.

Behaviour

It is all too common nowadays to hear about children with attention-deficit hyperactivity disorder (ADHD), which has a number of common behavioural traits, including restlessness, lack of concentration, sleep issues and constant agitation and motion. In this manifestation, we see all of the transitions in play: the child doesn't have enough essential fatty acids or phospholipids to help the central nervous system seal the small intestine; the sodium–potassium imbalance hyper-fires the adrenals and creates agitation; and there has been an incomplete copper–zinc transition, which is affecting the child's sleeping patterns and consequently its concentration, behaviour and co-dependency.

In these cases, it is vital to review the child's diet and lifestyle and ask what is over-challenging the body and what is happening as a result.

Diet is often the most obvious culprit here, because it is quite common in children with these extreme behavioural manifestations that the small intestine hasn't properly sealed and protein molecules of gluten and dairy are escaping into the bloodstream and moving on to the brain, triggering the behavioural disorder there.

Many behavioural issues are thought to be related to psychology rather than biochemistry, but when we start to study the lives of previous generations and see the issues that are being carried through, even just in terms of increased dehydration, lack of cleansing and inflammation, it can be seen that they all build up and create challenges for the child and parents, particularly if they are not resolved before puberty.

If, on the other hand, we can resolve issues in childhood, we can release stress and create freedom of movement, which will be highly beneficial during puberty.

PUBERTY

Puberty can be a difficult and demanding time, and what happens during it has a key influence over our long-term health. Unfortunately, if childhood issues have not been resolved, and the body is not able to hold a great deal of light, puberty can be a dark place, quite literally. It is perhaps unsurprising that many teenagers look for artificial means of coping and stimulation in order to feel good, e.g. caffeine, alcohol, nicotine, recreational drugs and a less-than-optimal diet high in sugars and saturated fats.

The Knowledge to Make Informed Decisions

Modern advances in medicine, technology and lifestyle have many pitfalls for the unaware during puberty. For example, the HPV vaccine, the cervical cancer vaccine, is offered to girls of 12, and it is not uncommon for them to be given hormonal contraceptives as well. What saddens and worries me is that, at such a young age, they may not understand their full story in terms of connectedness or realize how vulnerable they may be. For example, if a girl is born with many inherited predispositions and, say, zinc availability is a little difficult, then the HPV vaccine and/or hormonal contraceptives will further reduce her levels of zinc and may affect her fertility later on in life. Unfortunately, I see this scenario played out all too often in women who go on to suffer with conditions such as polycystic ovaries, fibroids and fertility issues.

There has also been some interesting research into schizophrenia, conducted by Dr Carl Pfeiffer, an American physician and biochemist, which demonstrates that blood group A people have more difficulty keeping their zinc levels in balance. From this study, we can conclude that a blood group A girl will be more vulnerable than other girls to zinc imbalances when taking the contraceptive pill, because it excretes zinc from the body. And if we take this story of the blood group A girl a bit further, we can see how this one decision can play out throughout her life. Let's say, for example, that her background is full of predispositions and that she decides to take the contraceptive pill during puberty, then, later in her 20s, wishes to have a baby. Even if we just look at the zinc picture, we can see that she may have issues around her fertility or that her children may be susceptible to eczema.

We all want to make the right decisions at this important time in our life, but without knowledge we are disempowered. For example, one of my children was the only one of 25 students who chose not to have the meningitis vaccine when she was at college. Everyone was really curious to know why she didn't want the vaccine, and understood when she explained her reasons.

The problem is that we are kept in the dark about so many of the potential dangers of modern life, and young people in particular need to be able to make informed choices. They need to know their background and the predispositions they have inherited, so that they can think in a connected way about their potential for receiving and transmitting light throughout their lifetime.

Predispositions and Vulnerabilities

Puberty is one of the most amazing times in life, but it is also when we are very vulnerable, and this is partly due to the fact that our teenage years are usually the most reckless times of our lives – when we are more likely to eat too many fast foods, sugars and processed foods, drink too much and perhaps take recreational drugs or smoke, with little idea (or care) about the consequences.

We are also vulnerable to the so-called must-haves of modern life. Hormonal contraceptives, vaccines and medical treatments often disrupt our natural balance, while technological advances such as mobile phones, Wi-Fi and computers all negatively affect our potential for full health. I find it particularly worrying that so many of these devices are kept in the bedroom or are in constant use. Why? To put it very simply, they are electromagnetic pollutants and create a lot of stress for us, as we are electromagnetic beings ourselves. So we contract rather than relax and flow, and we are less open to the universal rhythms that keep us in harmony and in company with the other human beings on the planet. Company is more important than we might think – being on the end of a phone or a computer seems to me to be a manner of dropping out from society rather than fully engaging with it.

As a result of all this electromagnetic living, our condition at the end of puberty can be absolutely devastated and set the scene for the rest of our life.

The Picture at the End of Puberty

By the end of puberty we have a thumbnail sketch, if you like, of the story so far and of the likely story in the future. Looking at a person's picture at the end of puberty often explains why certain issues arise when they are between 40 and 50, or 40 and 60, years of age. It's almost as if the blueprint of potential settles in us at that time.

This makes sense because by this time brain development and growth have been completed, and so has the way that the brain operates – the balance, or lack of balance, between right and left hemispheres. Also, there will be strong indicators of a person's approach and ability to fulfil their potential, and whether the cells are operating in a full aerobic way and benefiting from a good supply of oxygen or moving in a slightly more anaerobic way and struggling. So, when we look at what is happening in a person's life between the ages of 16 and 19, we can see a strong, almost psychedelic, picture of their potential and their weaknesses.

Looking at a person's life at the end of puberty also enables us to see the way they fit in between heaven and Earth. From now on, they're going to move forward as an adult. Are they in a position to express who they are and reach their full potential? Or have some of the transitional stages been impaired, so that life will have to offer up more dramatic scenarios in order for them to resolve the issues that have been inherited or created?

Mental Health

Finally, a word about mental health, because a person's mental health at the end of puberty can affect their later potential for health, and an alarming number of young people nowadays suffer with eating disorders or mental health issues.

I quite often find that where a young daughter has eating distress, there is also a son in the family with mental health issues. More than 40 years of looking at these stories has indicated to me that certain things must be in the background of these young people.

Books have been written around eating distress and theories put forward suggesting that, for example, 'both parents of an anorexic will be alcoholics'. Although I don't believe this will be the true picture, it doesn't negate the fact that alcoholic parents will predispose a child to have a strong liver picture, and similarly, those suffering with mental health disorders are quite often coeliac from birth, i.e. they cannot tolerate gluten in the diet, which is usually an inherited predisposition. Therefore, it's important that we understand out ancestry, where we've come from and what has gone on in the lives of our parents and grandparents – our whole story.

For example, we know the highest incidence of schizophrenia in the world is found on the west coast of Ireland, and that area also has the highest incidence of coeliac disease, which, if untreated, can lead to schizophrenia. If the small intestine is healthy, the area of absorption is the area of a soccer pitch, but if the villi, the little protuberances that create this huge absorptive area, are not developed or lying down, then the absorption area becomes much smaller. The problem is that a person can move through childhood without this issue being noticed, but come the demands of puberty, it takes its toll.

CASE STUDY

Picture a person who wasn't breastfed and therefore didn't get the mother's colostrum, so the copper–zinc balance wasn't rectified in infancy, and the essential fatty acids and phospholipids weren't administered, which caused a leakage of protein molecules through the wall of the small intestine.

This issue continued through childhood, perhaps manifesting as eczema or another skin condition at first – the body saying 'I'm under stress, I'm uncomfortable, I'm irritated and I'm inflamed.' Or perhaps the child was affected by ADHD or sleep problems.

Suppressed or unresolved, the issues moved deeper and impacted the lungs and, as a consequence, depression set in, or the person became lower in spirits than they would have been if they had been expressing their true nature.

If, in addition, the contraceptive pill or recreational drugs were taken throughout the teenage years, the issue may have moved from the lungs to the mind, manifesting in depression or eating distress, for example, or more serious mental conditions. The severity of the issues would depend upon the levels of depletion in the person's background.

All of these issues are actually symptoms that tell us that the situation may become more serious, or even life-threatening, by the end of puberty. What future does this person have ahead of them?

NOTHING HAPPENS BY CHANCE

So far we've explored all of the things that undermine our ability to reach our light-holding potential in adulthood: our predispositions and our way of life from preconception through childhood and the teenage years.

Unfortunately, modern medical treatments often simply serve to accelerate our weaknesses rather than effect a cure. Rather than seeing early illnesses as signs asking us to take notice of the stress the body is under, and to make simple changes to resolve the issues, we ignore or, worse, suppress the symptoms and then the issues go deeper into the body.

Of course these vulnerabilities can be resolved, but only if there is awareness and then knowledge about how to change. Everything is connected, but most people don't see the connections. But understanding all the body's predispositions at the end of puberty allows us to have joined-up thinking in terms of our potential.

How can we maximize that potential?

Chapter 4

Understanding
What Cures Us

How do we bring the body back into balance? How do we cure our issues and dis-eases?

In order to find a cure, first we need to rectify a general misunderstanding about the mechanics of healing. Most people have a belief that a cure comes from outside themselves, rather than from themselves as part of a greater universal plan, which means that we are part of the disease *and* the cure.

Modern medicine, and consequently our beliefs about disease, stem from Louis Pasteur's theories about disease. According to these theories, we have particular symptoms, a particular disease, because we have caught a virus or picked up certain bacteria, which are working within our body, creating morbid matter. If not resolved by medical intervention, this situation could maim or kill us. Following on from this, we believe that germs, bacteria, viruses and microbes are our natural enemies and seek to suppress any symptoms of disease with pharmaceutical products.

This is what the medical profession has led us to believe is the correct course of action, but it's important to realize that although medical progress has improved our health in many ways, we can also say that the foundations of modern medicine are flawed.

When Pasteur was working, in the 19th century, microscopes were not powerful enough to either prove or disprove his theories, although their results were convincing enough to launch a huge pharmaceutical industry, which continues to create more and more pills, potions and processes to kill off bacteria and viruses – antibiotics, antivirals, anti-inflammatories, etc. These treatments may make us feel better by suppressing the symptoms, but they are not a cure.

The problem is that this method of treatment doesn't take into account the hierarchy of symptoms that might be present in a person's story. For example, a person might experience some non-threatening inflammation – a natural healing process – but antibiotics cut that short. So, rather than resolve the issue (as would have happened naturally), this results in an increased build-up of toxicity. As we learned earlier, if you suppress a symptom, it simply goes deeper.

What is the answer? Fortunately, Pasteur wasn't the only microbiologist looking at germ theory. The work of Béchamp, Rife and Naessens diametrically opposed Pasteur's theories and offered an alternative view: a perspective of the body as healer. They said that healing came from within rather than from commercially viable pills, potions and creams.

Antoine Béchamp didn't believe that bacteria invaded a healthy host and created disease, as his research indicated that the body actually created the bacteria in response to the condition of the host and to environmental factors. Advocates of Béchamp's work maintain that his experiments were more detailed than Pasteur's because he used a much more powerful microscope and so was able to see how living entities — tiny soluble ferments, infinitely smaller than cells — influenced the way cells or tissues operated. He called these ferments 'microzymes' and found them in all organic substances. He theorized that these tiny forms were more basic to life than the cells themselves and considered them to be the building blocks of living matter, responsible for how cells and tissues and organs and whole living organisms behaved from a physiological and biochemical perspective. He believed them to be the seeds of life.

Béchamp also found that if you put microzymes into different solutions, representing different conditions in the body, this resulted in different sets of so-called germs. His experiments were detailed and thorough and provide a complete perspective on disease, indicating that it is the human body itself that decides how things work in it — which puts us firmly in control of our health. However, Pasteur's competing vision became widely accepted by scientists, and Béchamp's research sank into obscurity. On his deathbed Pasteur did say he was wrong and the work of Béchamp was correct, but by then it was too late – the pharmaceutical industry had been set in motion and the warfare against microbes had begun.

Even before Béchamp's time, the ancient Greek physician Hippocrates spoke about humours, which relate to the extracellular fluids. How these are nurtured and developed clearly influences the body's health.

The work of Royal Raymond Rife, an American inventor and early exponent of the high-magnification time-lapse cinemicrograph, was also instrumental in the understanding of disease, as he developed a microscope in the 1920s that was able to offer significantly increased magnification and, more importantly, didn't kill the specimen. The increased magnification meant that Rife was able to prove that germs could not be the source of disease; they could only be the result. Furthermore, he was able to measure the exact frequency of the light coming from cells and found that if you then fed this light back to them, their condition could be changed instantly. In other words, all the changes that resulted in health or disease were taking place inside these micro-organisms, for which Rife used Dr Wilhelm Reich's term, 'bions'.

Like Béchamp, Rife also noticed a 16-step change that occurred when a micro-organism was moved into another medium (environment), and realized that these changes meant that the frequency of the organism changed, which meant the frequency of light changed, too. He was then able to experiment with how different, very specific light frequencies impacted micro-organisms.

There was a revival of interest in Rife's work in the 1980s and a group of scientists have since rebuilt his microscope. During his lifetime, however, he was persecuted and, like Béchamp before him, ridiculed and opposed.

Gaston Naessens, a French biologist, also developed a new optical microscope, in his case in the 1950s, although he wasn't aware of Rife's invention. Using this microscope, he was able to isolate the light frequency from tiny micro-organisms that he called 'somatids'. He realized, like Béchamp and Rife, that these micro-organisms were pretty indestructible, and again noted a form-changing cycle. Rife documented 16 stages and Naessens 15, but both mentioned 16 separate forms.

We are taught to believe that these forms are bacterial from the outside, but Naessens' research indicated that the bacteria were produced by the morbid matter, or the malfunctioning of tissue. In resolving the issue, the cell forms these bacteria as part of the disease process – they are there to resolve a challenging situation. The same thing is true of viruses, mycobacteria or mycelia (the vegetative parts of a fungus) – they are all part of the 16-step process that the body uses to find resolution to issues within the cells, to move from a dis-eased state back to real health.

I believe that most people, including those in the medical profession, are looking in the wrong direction for a cure to disease. Naessens also proved that DNA is not the independent ruler of life, as we've been taught, but is built from what comes before it, i.e. the environmental, vibrational, energetic state and the inherited predispositions to certain health issues.

The idea of predisposition is supported by Dr Lawrence Broxmeyer's research into the 1918–19 flu pandemic, which affected 500 million people worldwide. In a recent article he revealed that although the flu virus could create an epidemic, it doesn't have the virulence to create a pandemic. Broxmeyer's research indicates that the 'flu victims' in that pandemic actually died from tuberculosis (TB). What he discovered was that they were carrying TB as a vulnerability – a predisposition.

THE LINK BETWEEN ACUTE EPISODES AND CHRONIC DISEASES

Now we can begin to understand how the constantly changing forms discovered by Béchamp, Rife and Naessens affect the state of play within our body. These forms, or microzymas, in the extracellular fluids are a vital part of the healing process, as they are agents of change within the cells, having the ability to transform into bacteria or viruses and support the body as required.

We already know that when the body needs to resolve an issue – for example, when the pH balance has become too acidic – there will be a short-lived acute episode (classically lasting three days), perhaps a sore throat and a raised temperature. This acute episode creates inflammation and heat, which allows the body to clear the stagnation and return the tissue to normality. At this point in the process, the microzymas are no longer required in a bacterial or viral form, so they return to a symbiotic form.

The problem is that people are fearful of acute episodes and seek to suppress them, with antibiotics or anti-inflammatories for example, which means that the original issue remains unresolved. We know that if these acute episodes continue to be suppressed, the issue will be driven deeper into the body and eventually go down to join the chronic toxic load. Sadly, it will often turn up in later life as arthritis or asthma or changes of bowel, liver or lung function and be labelled a 'chronic disease' because it will go on and on.

When looking at case histories, I often find this link between acute episodes and chronic diseases. For example, someone diagnosed with ME will often have experienced many acute episodes, such as sore throats or ear infections, and maybe flu-like symptoms as a child, but as they have grown older, these have stopped and they may not have experienced any acute episodes for many years. They may feel they are free of the problem, but in fact their body has lost the energy, freedom and movement to clear the issue by creating inflammation.

This is why it is so much more difficult to resolve a chronic disease. But *it is possible*, and is usually achieved by releasing the movement and energy to allow inflammation and acute episodes to take place again. (*For more on this, see the Appendix.*)

It's important to understand that acute episodes can be nursed without suppressing the symptoms, and that they are part of the body's natural defences against chronic disease. I believe that this knowledge is so valuable that it should be passed on from one generation to the next. It is part of understanding and living in symbiosis with the body's natural patterns of healing.

During the spring and autumn equinoxes, for example, there is a huge surge of energy in the body. These are very specific times, because they mark the changeovers between winter and summer. During the winter our energy primarily moves up our back and down our front, but at the spring equinox this circulation flips and the energy then moves up our front and down our back, which has a much more expansive feel. At the autumn equinox our flow of energy again reverses. This is a natural shift from the opening, expansive time of summer into the closing, introspective time of winter. It means that twice a year our cells experience a natural detoxifying event. This is why many people tend to get colds or flu around the times of the equinoxes. When the body experiences this sudden, sharp change of direction of energy, there is a discharge of toxicity; it moves into the lymph and drains into the blood, and is then filtered by the liver and out of the body.

While I was working with a medical practitioner, I noticed that after an equinox there would be an influx of patients in the waiting room with acute episodes. This pattern should have been a good thing, because these natural detoxifying events have the ability to burn off some of our chronic load. However, I noticed that if these acute episodes were suppressed instead of simply being carefully nursed, the issue would often appear later as a chronic manifestation. Issues such as arthritis, asthma, migraines or bowel disorders, for example, would worsen. As a result, many patients suppressed the issue further and several weeks after the equinox there would be a high demand for psychiatric services.

WISDOM AND HARMONY –
WITHIN AND WITHOUT

As a practitioner, my work has always been to help people get in touch with their inner wisdom. Once we understand our story, we understand the path that led us to illness. Disease occurs when we fall out of rhythm, as that diminishes our ability to hold light and produce light. Resolution happens when we tune in to our natural rhythms, return our body to the light and thereby achieve our full potential – the potential with which we were born.

The important thing to understand is that returning to the light doesn't rely on the opinions of others, or even a medical practitioner's diagnosis, but is entirely unique to each one of us. The problem is that most people, and the medical profession, believe that both the disease and the cure are found outside ourselves, and so we feel disempowered – as if we have no ability to influence what is going on, when the opposite is actually true. In my experience, however, it seems that many people would rather pop a pill to suppress their symptoms than find the cure. Perhaps changing their diet or way of being gets in the way of their lifestyle? Or they just don't know any better?

There is a bigger picture; we just have to open our eyes.

Chapter 5

The Tubercular
Pandemic

Looking at health on a collective level, one of the main issues facing us is what I call the tubercular pandemic.

Tuberculosis (TB) was only identified as a disease in the 19th century, but it has been known since ancient times. Tubercular decay has been found in the spines of Egyptian mummies.

As a thumbnail sketch, TB is the inability to keep calcium in the correct place. The body has an absolute need for calcium and will crave it when it is in short supply. Irish novels have described people eating the limewash off their walls in their desire for calcium. However, as with all minerals, it's the positioning of calcium that's as important as the availability. If it is in the wrong place, there will be an issue with blood sugar levels. One of the easiest ways of understanding blood sugar, as described by Martin Budd in his book *Low Blood Sugar*, is to think of it as consistent levels of calcium in the blood.

Therefore, a tubercular pandemic doesn't necessarily mean people manifesting TB, although we do know that in many places in the world, in particular India and Africa, people with HIV are suffering from TB, not AIDS (*see also page 76*). A tubercular pandemic is actually when the four all-important electrolytes – sodium, potassium, calcium and magnesium – move into the wrong position, resulting in dehydration and cellular contraction.

It's easy to picture the movement of calcium within the body because when something becomes calcified, or that lovely old word 'incalcitrant', it becomes so hardened and inflexible that it is difficult to move or change. This hardening process lowers a person's vibration and resonance and has a huge impact in terms of their connection to light.

We know from Béchamp's work that this 'tubercular taint' may be an inherited predisposition, and the microzymes do have the ability to change. This is why it is important that we have a clear understanding of our vulnerability to the TB taint.

THE METAL ELEMENT AND TB

The five elements of Chinese medicine are Wood, Fire, Earth, Metal and Water. Each corresponds to a time of the year, as well as certain organs and emotions, tastes, smells and sounds and a whole variety of other aspects. The five elements can help us to connect at deeper levels and make sense of what at first might seem unrelated emotions and events. The Metal element is incredibly helpful in understanding how the tubercular taint (or tubercular miasm, as homoeopaths call it, or the inherited Metal element in the causative factor of five element acupuncture) manifests within us, and moreover why it has become such a common occurrence.

First, it is important to understand that the body will always defend itself, following the hierarchy of organs. One of the lesser organs is the colon. This is our largest organ of elimination and is assigned the Metal element. As it can be thought of as a reservoir of fluids, it is the colon that will register if we're dehydrated. It has so many nerve endings that it is often referred to as the second brain. This ties in with water being the instrument of holding messages within the body. Normally, the colon holds, receives and transmits messages about the hydration of the body. However, if the tubercular taint is present, then it will diminish this vital function of the colon.

The lungs are also part of the Metal element, and the most common form of TB, pulmonary tuberculosis, manifests there and destroys the bronchial tissue. The lungs control the intake of *chi*, the intake of life – breathing in the light. The placement of electrolytes is important for the lungs, too, as sodium and calcium contract muscles, while potassium and magnesium relax and extend muscles. So, if calcium is misplaced due to the tubercular taint, it's going to influence the diaphragm and intercostal muscles and everything connected to the lungs. It's going to affect our breathing.

The lungs are also the seat of depression. If TB manifests, it causes a contraction in the body, reducing the water-holding capacity of the colon, and the resulting dehydration lowers the body's resonance. This contraction of the body denies the person full contact with light. The effects of this can be seen particularly clearly in sufferers of seasonal affective disorder (SAD) and also myalgic encephalopathy (ME). They often struggle to heal while they're living in the darker, colder northern hemisphere, but if they go somewhere warm and very light, they feel totally different.

When the tubercular taint is present, a person will already have a predisposition towards contraction and the inability to connect to the universal energies via light.

As we know, when an illness or imbalance is suppressed, it can progress from a less serious issue in a lower organ to a more serious issue in a higher organ – for example, from the skin and colon (e.g. eczema) to the lungs (e.g. asthma) – and that's when we can see the TB taint manifesting. Furthermore, the lungs have a large part to play in the state of being of a person, so when there is an imbalance there (which is also depicted as degrees of dehydration), it goes beyond them and reaches the mind.

A lack of light and hydration in the mind is bound to change behaviour – on a personal, social and worldwide level – and you can't escape the fact that mental health is a huge issue in modern society, so understanding our predisposition with regards to the TB taint is vital, because once we understand how to recognize it manifesting in the body, then we can take steps to remedy the situation and avoid more serious consequences. In thinking about our health, it's important to remember that what has been created can also be taken to pieces.

So, let's start by understanding how a predisposition to the TB taint manifests in its early stages, in the lesser organs, and progresses to the manifestation of more serious issues and diseases in the higher organs.

ADDICTION

This process is particularly apparent in the issue of addiction, where clearly the changes have reached the mind. However, it is unlikely that a manifestation of an issue like this at the brain level – the highest aspect of the central nervous system – could happen within one lifetime. The body is highly protective, so it is pretty inconceivable that in one lifetime a person could become strongly addicted to something that is doing them harm, even when earlier issues have been suppressed by pharmaceuticals. It is a more likely scenario that when we look at the previous generations, we will see an imbalance in the lungs, colon or skin – for example, in the lungs in depression or asthma, or tobacco smoking; in the colon, issues such as irritable bowel syndrome (IBS) or Crohn's disease; in the skin, manifestations such as psoriasis or eczema. If we look deeply enough, we're bound to see the microzymas changing, the displacement of electrolytes and a lowered resonance, creating a predisposition for more rigid posturing. This inheritance usually shows up vividly by the age of about 16, which is when addictive behaviour often starts.

The addiction may be a form of escapism from something so stressful and challenging that the person can't actually cope with it. There are a number of possible scenarios why addiction occurs, but think for a moment – if you took 20 people and introduced them to a substance, why would it be that a small percentage would become addicted and the rest would just experiment and then put it aside?

The case study below looks at three possible scenarios that, in my experience, often give rise to this manifestation of the inherited TB taint.

CASE STUDY

First, it is possible that the copper–zinc ratio remained unbalanced after the child was born. Mother Nature presents the perfect solution for rebalancing the zinc levels after birth, and all animals know this, but if the mother doesn't consume her placenta, then her colostrum and first milk won't provide sufficient zinc to restore her child's zinc–copper ratio, so it's not difficult to see how short of zinc many babies will be. This, in turn, will make the child more vulnerable to the tubercular taint, because the issue wasn't resolved in infancy.

Second, if the child's small intestine doesn't seal but remains porous after the age of two, because the child's diet (and that of the mother, if she is breastfeeding) lacks phospholipids and the right oils, then gluten and dairy protein molecules can pass out of the gut and cross the blood–brain barrier, which alters the way in which the brain functions. Unfortunately, this is a common occurrence in children today and, as we have seen, can lead to a number of digestive and skin issues, which, if suppressed, can go deeper into the lungs and then into the mind.

Third, there needs to be very healthy villi activity in the child to ensure a high absorption of nutrients. However, another common predisposition is gluten sensitivity. Thus, absorption is poor, but this often goes undetected and manifests as behavioural disorders of the central nervous system and at brain level.

These predispositions are all there to be seen in the person's story. They might also show up as:

- night terrors or poor sleep
- bowel imbalances
- skin manifestations
- particularly dependent behaviour

In choosing to be highly addicted to something that is detrimental, the body shows a lack of judgement in its own survival. Interestingly, in Eastern medicine the small intestine is considered to be the great separator of the pure from the impure, in terms of both food and judgement. Also, Eastern European chiefs used to say that to be a chief you need to be very independent, and to achieve this, to eat the eye and the testicles of an animal, because these organs are high in zinc. If you're choosing a chief, you're certainly not going to choose a dependent one, because they couldn't do the job properly. Balanced copper–zinc ratios, on the other hand, manifest someone who is not fearful but has good judgement – precisely the qualities needed in a chief.

There are, of course, biochemical differences within the three scenarios presented in the case study above. However, if we look back, keeping in mind that the microzymas can deteriorate generation by generation, we will understand the reasons why this predisposition (which some people call an addictive personality) is manifesting.

I consider addiction to be part of the tubercular pandemic because it is so rife now, with a huge number of late-teenagers dependent upon substances, and we know that high copper levels in the brain lead to this state of being.

ADHD

As mentioned in Chapter 3, attention-deficit hyperactivity disorder (ADHD) is on the increase. The tubercular taint is clearly part of this picture, too, when we look at the predisposing factors – for example, what was inherited from the child's grandparents' stories, parents' stories, the pregnancy and birth, and what stresses (including vaccines and weaning) the child experienced before the age of two.

Looking at cases like this, it seems to me a great pity that we have moved away from living collectively, where wise women or grandparents would pass on knowledge to a mother about how to nurture a child. This lack of connection on a societal level has had unfortunate consequences.

There is a real lack of soothing and peace in people with ADHD; they always look as if they're stressed. Interestingly, magnesium and calcium are known to be the soothers; they work in opposition in the movement in and out of the cells, but we need enough magnesium, which is a natural tranquillizer, to keep calcium in the correct place and maintain balanced blood sugar.

It is often the case with ADHD that the stress was already there in the child's lineage, and this predisposition was accentuated by the stress of weaning, as foods such as dairy and gluten can often be challenging. Depending on the seriousness of the condition, there might also be issues with a porous small intestine – did it fully seal or are food molecules getting into the bloodstream? If this is the case, it isn't unusual for the child to have night terrors – the level of stress and anxiety is stopping the child from sleeping. As mentioned earlier, an Epsom salts bath before sleep can be very beneficial in these circumstances, because magnesium sulphate is a natural tranquillizer.

It is also quite likely, depending on the lineage, that there will be a food absorption issue and the villi may be sensitive to wheat (but not necessarily all other glutinous grains). Elevated copper levels will aggravate the issue and the restlessness often manifests at skin level, so there may be skin sensitivities.

All these manifestations are interconnected, so it's important to know the person's full story to understand how and why the tubercular taint has manifested.

ANOREXIA AND EATING DISTRESS

Like addiction, anorexia, or any eating distress, isn't just going to come out of the blue, although that's how it may appear. In my experience, there is a most interesting connection between the BCG vaccination (TB vaccine) and anorexia. Among the young women (and usually their parents, too) who've consulted me about an eating disorder, 90 per cent of them developed it a short time after having the BCG vaccination. (Until recently, it was common practice to administer the vaccine at the onset of puberty, usually at the age of 12.) In these cases, I usually found that a strong tubercular taint had been passed down through the ancestral lineage and had manifested in the small intestine as coeliac disease. This predisposition, plus the vaccine and the great demands of puberty, had placed a huge amount of stress on the girls' central nervous system and so pushed the predisposition upwards – from their lungs to their mind.

There are two cases in my immediate family where this scenario happened: one occurred at the onset of puberty and the other at the end of puberty. Within six months of the BCG vaccine, both family members were seriously affected by anorexia.

The point is that the vaccine has the same resonance as the taint that's being carried through the lineage, and so the additional stress will result in the energy blueprint creating the physical biochemistry.

In treating anorexia, there is a particular difficulty, as, quite understandably, the parents just want the child to eat something and might press the idea of 'just a bit of toast or cereal' on them. However, if there is a coeliac picture in the story, gluten and certain oils will continue to jeopardize the recovery.

In all the conditions we've discussed – addictions, ADHD and anorexia – the blood–brain barrier is vital, because if it's not functioning properly, then issues in the lower hierarchy of organs will manifest in the brain at a later stage.

What's important to understand here is that all 'mental' conditions – motor neurone disease, for example, or Alzheimer's – are manifested in some way in childhood. For example, recurrent throat issues, eczema or lung infections indicate that the tubercular taint is present in the child's predisposition. The problem comes when, without realizing the consequences, the parents respond by suppressing the issue – for example with steroid creams or antibiotics – so the predisposition gets deeper or stronger.

In addition, remember that when the Metal element is in someone's story, the weakness starts with a degree of dehydration and contraction in the large intestine, is then pushed to the lungs and then, eventually, pushed to the light – the mind. These may be people who feel they have a slightly melancholic approach to life; they may be people who feel stress more than others.

It's so important to understand a person's whole story, including any predisposition to the tubercular taint. The tubercular pandemic is a huge crisis in our society, and stress is building up in society as a whole, too, because we're not living according to the natural laws – in our treatment of the Earth, food and lifestyle. Inevitably, this stress will be passed down from generation to generation as a physical manifestation; it will influence our cells, our resonance and our ability to be in touch with universal wisdom via light.

Chapter 6

More Examples of the Tubercular Inheritance

When considering anything at all about health, it is vital that we can see what is happening in our body as an energetic blueprint holding a specific resonance. Therefore, when an issue or disease manifests, it means that our body's resonance is discordant with the universal resonance, which is why we are in dis-ease. If we're not resonating in tune and in harmony with the cosmos, it's bound to create stress and fear; this changes our energetic blueprint and will result in a physical manifestation of some description.

KNOWLEDGE AND SELF-UNDERSTANDING

In the beginning of the human story, we would have heard every message from the universe because the Water element would have been intact and we would have been fully hydrated – there would have been no room for fear and anxiety. What we find now, however, is the more serious an illness, or the deeper it goes into the being of a person, i.e. touching mind, body or actually threatening life itself, the less intact the energetic hand-down, or the hydration. The blueprint for the liver, in which the fluids are perfectly balanced, is 80 per cent hydration of the brain and 70 per cent hydration of the body, but that level of hydration simply isn't there in most people. To restore that balance, it is vital to understand our story, our inheritance, our energetic blueprint. Then we will know how to correct the hydration issue.

It's always very interesting to see clients become empowered with this knowledge and self-understanding. Before they understand their story, their fear is tangible, but when they fully understand how it arose, what is going on now and how they themselves can change it, their energetic blueprint changes and they are able to reconfigure their physical manifestation according to this new energetic blueprint.

Today, many people have to face the most challenging sorts of diseases and conditions, such as AIDS or myalgic encephalomyelitis (ME), which, even if they're not an actual death sentence, are physically or mentally debilitating. Those suffering with these types of conditions are often at the extreme end of the energetic blueprint, by which I mean that the energy handed down their family line has been distorted, and this manifests in many different ways within the body.

First, the level of hydration changes, and this affects how the central nervous system functions, so these people will hold an enormous amount of fear and anxiety. We tend to think of people having to change the way they live in order to stop fear from coming in, but fear is generated equally from inside, as dehydrated cells hold a strong message of fear and anxiety.

Second, the 16 stages of energetic change that we spoke about earlier will be trying to resolve the situation, and so will manifest different properties or symptoms. Therefore, the person might experience a bacterial, viral, mycobacterial or mycelial infection in the body's attempt to resolve the imbalance and restore health.

I've picked out a common disease – AIDS – and a common condition – ME – to explain how these 16 changes might manifest in a person's story and lead up to these serious diseases in the body.

ME (Myalgic Encephalomyelitis)

My experience is that there is huge frustration among sufferers of ME because many people, including medical doctors, say the condition does not exist. ME sufferers experience total and utter exhaustion, but the pace of modern life can be exhausting, so what is so different about ME?

ME doesn't just manifest in physical tiredness. The sorts of issues that arise fairly consistently in case histories of ME are that it has reached the person's lungs, in their lack of energy, but also there is a feeling of lowness and a degree of disconnectedness in the mind and body.

The issue that almost always shows up is bowel function. The most common issue is irritable bowel syndrome (IBS), which may have occurred in the past or still be current when the person is manifesting all the symptoms of ME. IBS is a strong indication of dehydration. It indicates that the colon is no longer able to hold that full-capacity message for the nerve endings that tells a person: 'I'm fully hydrated, therefore I'm not anxious, I'm at peace with the world.'

In many people, the IBS has been preceded by ear infections or throat infections in childhood. We have seen that the ear, being the orifice of the kidneys, is an early indication of dehydration and lack of ability to cleanse and move the lymph, so these areas of inflammation and heat (the ear infections) are the body's natural way of clearing toxicity. When this natural resolution process is cut short by antibiotics, of course the clearing doesn't happen and a high level of dehydration and toxicity remains in the body, continuing to create internal stress.

Equally, this natural detoxification might have manifested as throat infections. The throat is a prime area for lymph stagnation. Again, suppressing these infections rather than letting the issue be resolved during childhood will prevent the natural flow of hydration from taking place and the issue will move deeper into the body.

Particularly in the early stages of life, mild ear or throat infections signal that there is a problem with the sinuses or higher lungs, which is likely to have arisen because of a less-than-optimal diet. In all things, diet is vital. Throughout our life our diet needs to serve five main purposes in order to create optimal cellular health. It needs to maintain:

- the highest level of hydration
- an alkaline body (remembering that all of the bodily functions are acid-forming, it is particularly important that our nutrition and lifestyle allow us to maintain the alkaline state)
- the correct body temperature
- electron–photon storage
- maximum oxygen availability

Moving into the pubescent years, this is when our lifestyle is often at its most hectic and unhealthy, as most people tend to indulge in a bit too much drinking, too many late nights and perhaps a poor diet – and it may be then that IBS begins to build or manifest. Again, if this issue is not resolved, it will just continue inside the body, building up more and more stress until ultimately other stresses overload the body and ME manifests.

What we need to remember is that many people will identify with this story, but for a high percentage, this situation will not manifest ME. The important difference is that the person who goes on to develop ME is carrying a predisposition that has built up through the generations – an energetic blueprint, a tubercular taint.

A surprising but consistent sign of the tubercular inheritance in ME is often overcrowded teeth. The reason people have overcrowded teeth is not because nature designed the teeth to be too big for the person's jaw, but because there is a blueprint that has been passed down. Ideally, the two sides of the upper palate should come together and close quite early in baby's gestation, at around five months. Once the palate has come together, it continues to push downwards on the roof of the mouth, pushing the mouth outwards to create a good open bite, which is not an acute half-circle but has plenty of space for the teeth to grow into. If the palate doesn't come together at all, this is known as a cleft palate, but there are also all the stages in between, and a high palate is seen to be an issue in tubercular inheritance, as it indicates a misplacement of minerals and information in the energetic blueprint being handed down to the child.

When the mouth has a perfect open bite, with the roof pushed down to the lower jaw and all the teeth fitting well, the occipital at the back of the neck is relaxed and the referencing of the other parts of the skull to the rest of the body will work in perfect harmony. If the upper palate doesn't form to create an open bite, then there will be changes in the structure of the whole skull. What I find so frequently in ME is that there is an issue with the occipital area; there is tension where the head joins the neck, which restricts the energy flow between the two parts at the same level as the thyroid gland. As a result, there can be exhaustion in the thyroid and adrenals.

Everything is connected, so once you see this part of the story, you automatically know where to look next. ME, that deep exhaustion, happens when there is a predisposition to exterior and interior stress and is triggered by the different events and emotions that happen in life.

AIDS (Acquired Immune Deficiency Syndrome)

As the severity of a diagnosis increases, the level of fear rises. It matches the level of fear that is already being demonstrated within the person. What if AIDS signifies a complete collapse of the immune system? There are many reasons why this can happen. Over the years, many people with an AIDS diagnosis have come to me wanting to understand their story, so I've come to know the sort of issues that will be present even before meeting them.

It is almost always the case that we find TB – the actual disease – manifested in the person's ancestry. If the person affected was taken to heal in the very clear light of the mountains, this could have been treated successfully, and so the TB taint could have been removed from the energetic blueprint of the family line. However, this wasn't usually the case, and often a high level of susceptibility is passed down.

So we are likely to have a person who already has a very strong predisposition to the TB taint.

Whatever the issue, there is always a predisposition for weakness in the Metal element that plays out through the family line. For example, the mother is an alcoholic or had a similar addiction before and throughout the pregnancy, or there is addiction going back in the ancestry, or depression or asthma manifests somewhere along the family line.

Someone with TB in their family line will inevitably be predisposed to bacterial infections being thrown up by the body from time to time to resolve toxic matter. The body doesn't know how to work against us, so it tries to clear the issue by getting the lymph moving and so create a strong immune system. The problem, as we know, is that so-called modern Western ways of medicine abort that process by suppressing it so that it can't be fully resolved. Therefore, the majority of people manifesting AIDS have experienced multiple infections that have been suppressed, in addition to having a very strong predisposition to TB from their ancestral lines (usually two lines from the parentage). In homoeopathy we will often talk about a 'quadruple tubercular miasm', meaning that each of the four grandparents brings that predisposition, and in coming together they create a story of bacterial infections in the following generations.

If these bacterial attempts by the body to clear toxins keep being suppressed, ultimately they may change to become viral or fungal activity. Fungal manifestations, such as thrush and athlete's foot, are incredibly widespread in modern life. A fungal manifestation is an important sign in our story because it indicates that the cells in the body are beginning to become less aerobic. As we discussed earlier, the perfect cell will produce 80 per cent of its energy (ATP) from oxygen and 20 per cent from glucose. But when it is operating anaerobically, it can change to the point where ultimately the 80/20 ratio is reversed, meaning that there is a lack of oxygen for the functioning of the cell, and we see this scenario played out in AIDS.

CASE STUDY

Two issues that are unfortunately likely to result in the end of life in AIDS are pneumonia and Wilson's syndrome. Pneumonia obviously affects the person at the lung level, and has a strong tubercular taint beneath it, but Wilson's syndrome can lead to dementia, which means the tubercular taint has moved beyond the lungs and into the mind.

In ME, the tubercular picture manifests as exhaustion of the adrenals and thyroid, and with Wilson's syndrome, the thyroid is also affected. Specifically, it is not converting the T4 hormone to T3, which leads to a lowering of body temperature.

So, AIDS is where conditions in the test tube have changed severely: hydration is very poor, leading to fear and anxiety and resulting in damage to the central nervous system. The pH is acidic, creating all sorts of viral and fungal infections, and the body temperature is reduced, which means the thyroid isn't functioning properly. The ultimate damage is at a cellular level, as the electrons and photons exchange is very low and the flow of oxygen and light to the cells is poor.

It is important to remember that if someone succumbs to AIDS, it will be due to having this high predisposition, and it is widely observed that many of the people in the world who are allegedly dying from AIDS are actually dying from TB.

RAISING THE RESONANCE

The problem is that all the illnesses discussed in this chapter are perceived by our society with great seriousness and fear, and this constrains our ability to resolve them because the fear comes from without as well as within. It might even be true to say that the fear is more dangerous than any of the diseases in themselves, because it lowers our resonance, our dance with the universe, and, consequently, our receptivity. However, we know that the energetic blueprint within us, our 'energy body', is so responsive that understanding can lead to a change in the level of resonance, raising it to more movement, more connection, and the physical manifestation can change.

This is why the resonance therapies are so fascinating. In homoeopathy, particularly, it is very noticeable that the more work that is done for the hydration of a person, the quicker and easier the homoeopathy manifests healing.

Unfortunately, many distinguished practitioners and researchers of resonance have experienced ridicule and oppression, as have their therapies. For example, the Tesla therapy, the Tesla resonance machine, the Rife resonance machine, Beck's zapper, and more recently, sonar. Those great men, Rife, Tesla and Naessens, really understood that our health is configured around our resonance, our blueprint, and our journey is to raise our resonance, to stay in touch. The Schumann resonance, named after Winfried Otto Schumann, who measured global electromagnetic resonance, indicates that the Earth's resonance is speeding up – Schumann was able to predict this phenomenon mathematically in 1952 – and so we have to work really hard now to stay in touch with that, to manifest that high-speed resonance.

By and large, Western medicine isn't resolving acute illnesses and answering the issues of the tubercular inheritance. However, understanding our story, our energetic blueprint, and then interpreting the signs given by the body can help avoid all these illnesses. We'll also look at techniques to resolve them in the Appendix. For the moment, all we need to understand is that when there is a strong predisposition coming down from previous generations, we will have a predisposition to inherit it. If we then also lose our connection energetically, we will lose the ability to manifest our full potential in full consciousness.

The way forward starts with self-knowledge, because from that point we begin to understand how it is possible to raise the resonance of our body and mind, reduce our toxic and chronic load and so change our energetic blueprint. The key is knowing – and being – who we truly are.

Chapter 7

The Stress of Not Being Who We Truly Are

In our society, most people tend to think of stress as something that comes from outside – perhaps from a partner or other relationship, their job, lifestyle, finances, and so on. We might even say there are endless external forces that add to our stress load. We also know how we feel when we are under pressure or stressed – fearful, nervous, irritable and so on. However, we don't often stop to consider how these unresolved emotions are stored.

Remember that if the resonance of stress is held on the Water element for two years, the cell membrane will become compromised, due to the cholesterol impregnation. The body will also have registered the resonance of stress and started the process of dehydration alert.

THE DEHYDRATION ALERT

The dehydration alert is an expression of adaptation – the body adapts as part of its preservation-of-life process – but it results in both external and internal stress. As well as the external stress resulting in a loss of fluid, there will also be a diminution of the cellular fluid exchange to the outside, and this will create internal stress. Soon there can be a vicious circle going on where stress creates dehydration and dehydration creates further stress.

But that's not the end of the story because we know the health of the cell membrane is critical in order for the body to clear the cells completely of any unwanted metabolites every 24 hours, which means by the time we wake up in the morning each day we should be alkaline. However, if there is a defence mechanism occurring and the cell membrane is coated in cholesterol, this daily detoxification is not going to happen fully.

Neither is transmutation, because the dehydration alert means that the body is not attracting enough oxygen and photons of light for it to take place. Stress is expressed as a weakening of the cell membrane's potential, so we won't be carrying a very strong positive charge on the outer side of the membrane and will have difficulty attracting the clouds of electrons.

Highly regarded German pharmacologist and writer Dr Johanna Budwig, and other respected practitioners in this field, say that the more people can live their life being true to themselves, the larger their electron clouds will be, and therefore the larger the amount of photon energy they will be able to trap, which in turn will attract very good supplies of oxygen.

This, of course, is the perfect situation, but let's look further at what happens when all is not well.

COULD WE ALL BE GOING MOULDY?

We know that if everything is in perfect order, 80 per cent of our cells' ATP will be produced from oxygen and 20 per cent from glucose. This is the most highly efficient way that our cells can operate. We also know that our predispositions, passed down through the generations, will mean there is likely to be a level of hardening and dehydration in our inherited energetic blueprint. Unless extensive work is done preconceptually, this blueprint will be carried forward and expressed in the 16 different stages of the microzyma, the minute particles that influence cell make-up and functioning.

The cell functions perfectly when it has the ability to flow backwards and forwards through those 16 stages, and this is how it was at the beginning of humanity's story. However, nowadays our predispositions and toxic load mean that our cell functioning starts from lower down the marker of those stages. So we are not going to produce our energy from 80 per cent oxygen and 20 per cent glucose, but from somewhere along that scale.

What happens when there is less oxygen available to the cell? Take a moment to think of a very unhealthy cell. What state will it be in? It will be very dehydrated, the pH will be acidic, the electron clouds surrounding it will be sparse and/or drifting away from the cell, and the photon activity will be impaired. It will eventually reach a state that we call 'energy sparing' – meaning its energy will be produced from 80 per cent glucose, because there will only be 20 per cent oxygen available. It's easy to see that this cell is moving towards a completely anaerobic state, and of course tissue cannot exist anaerobically. We require oxygen not only for energy but for life itself.

If we cast our mind back to acute illnesses, where the body is throwing up inflammation, activity and a temperature in order to resolve a collection of toxicity, we can see the importance of energy. The cell needs energy and movement to pass the toxicity build-up through the lymph and the blood and out of the body. If we abort, suppress or stop the transition from toxicity to clarity, we create dehydration and stagnation.

It is easy to imagine the further stress this will put on the functioning of the body, and how it will affect the energetic blueprint we pass on. This is why our cells don't have the oxygenation potential they had generations ago.

And this is why I ask if we could all be going mouldy. Everybody reading this will know about candida, bloating, acidic conditions, aches and pains and so on. These issues can only occur if our cells are moving to a less aerobic situation. It appears that, collectively, this is what is happening. In fact, the spread of fungal activity is becoming quite alarming. Researchers such as Naessens, Rife and Béchamp noticed that it was when the microzyma reached the 16th, final, stage that the ferments in the extracellular fluids were mycelial, which is mouldy or fungal.

So, collectively we are becoming more sluggish, more stagnant, lowering our resonance, lowering our vibration and hardening. And we don't do anything about it because of fear. Fear and dehydration go together, and the result is stagnation. This stops us from being who we truly are, which brings further stress, and down we go in a vicious spiral.

HOW THIS STAGNATION IS EXPRESSED

Individually, there are many different levels at which we might be affected. There are levels of dehydration and interruption of energy that might manifest as constipation or irritable bowel syndrome, or an expression of the skin, or there could be deeper issues affecting the lungs, liver, etc. What I've done here is briefly pick out three conditions where the changes are much more extreme at the cellular level, affecting the hydration; the pH; the temperature and the electron, photon and oxygen situation.

Motor Neurone Disease

This is a rare condition that progressively damages the nervous system, causing the muscles to malfunction. It manifests when the motor neurone nerves stop working properly and affects everyday activities such as walking, speaking, breathing and swallowing.

In Western medicine, motor neurone disease is believed to be due to a build-up of toxicity, possibly from pesticides, etc. Exposure to high toxicity will lead to the body attempting to resolve the situation and, as we know, if this is suppressed rather than resolved, the toxicity will go deeper into the body. To give an example, I knew a lady who suffered with terrible migraines whenever she was exposed to the pesticide spraying of the barley on her farm. For years, she left the farm during the spraying. As she grew older, by chance she found that the spraying didn't cause her to have migraines any longer, so she stayed on the farm during the spraying. Her body was no longer throwing up the symptom that could have helped resolve the issue, however, and much later in life she developed motor neurone disease.

In this situation we know things have changed remarkably in the cells, to the point where the muscles are not being oxygenated. We also know that the blood–brain barrier has not been defending the higher aspect of the body: the brain. Remember that for the blood–brain barrier to operate well, we need iodine, vitamin D3 from sunlight and the DHA from omega 3. Therefore, a combination of nutritional imbalances and exposure to high toxicity can create this situation in which the nerves that control muscles can no longer operate as intended.

Autism Spectrum Disorders

Brain function is again affected in autism spectrum disorders. This may be a predisposition that is carried in the family — for example, there may be strong predispositions in all four grandparents. The transitions after birth — the copper–zinc rebalancing, the sodium–potassium switch and sealing of the small intestine — are all important in protecting the brain, particularly because the human brain develops more after birth than during gestation. In autism spectrum disorders it is common to see blood–brain barrier issues and, in particular, an elevated copper level.

We know too that with autism there is a high level of dehydration, because the central nervous system is affected. This situation means there is a high level of fear in people. They might have night terrors, be phobic and be very fixed around eating habits, going to strange places, making eye contact, etc.

I don't believe that autism spectrum disorders just happen; they build up over generations, resulting in autism being expressed in a particular person's life. From my experience, looking at the predispositions, the gestational period, the birth, infancy, childhood and what happened around the transitions, it is common to see stagnation of the Water element and a lack of clearing. So it's no surprise that high mercury and other heavy metals have been found in the tissues of people with autism spectrum disorders.

Eating Distress

Eating distress is now so rife, particularly among young women, but increasingly among men, too, that we have to question why it is affecting so many seemingly healthy people.

There usually has to be a strong predisposition for it to manifest and, as I have often seen in case histories, very much a tubercular taint, which means the person has great difficulty keeping calcium in the correct place.

The cell-functioning marker will be somewhere along the 16 stages; therefore, we won't have the 'perfect picture' of 80 per cent oxygen and 20 per cent glucose to start with, and there will be a certain amount of stagnation. It is generally acknowledged that zinc deficiency is present in those with eating distress, and there is also an increase of copper activity in the brain, so there is a strange electrical impulse or inflammation, which means things change in how the brain functions, too. We know that from a very young age there will be issues with the small intestine, with porosity leading to leakage of protein molecules and possibly coeliac disease. Earlier, I mentioned the common link I've seen between eating distress in girls and schizophrenia in the same family, usually a brother, and how I've noticed that the incidence of anorexia manifesting within six months of the BCG vaccine given at the onset of puberty. So this small intestinal story concerning coeliac disease and intestine porosity is definitely going to be there, along with the copper–zinc story, which will result in dehydration and changes in how the ATP is made, which in turn will affect the blood sugar and the function of the blood–brain barrier.

Here, I think it's also important to draw attention to the importance of iodine in healthy thyroid function, because this mineral is vital for the blood–brain barrier and the healthy functioning of all the cells in the body. Also, when a strong tubercular taint is running in a person, it usually means issues with how the thyroid functions, often Wilson's syndrome, with symptoms including fatigue, headaches, PMS, hair loss, irritability, fluid retention, depression, decreased memory, low sex drive and easy weight gain. This is due to a shortage of iodine, but also difficulty in converting T4 to T3. A further problem is that conventional blood tests are not necessarily accurate in showing how the thyroid is functioning. I haven't yet come across a manifestation of eating distress in a case history that has reached head level without issues with the thyroid showing up, often about five years before the eating distress fully manifested.

It is vital to understand how stress is expressed in our cells – both the changes and the sorts of illnesses that can be manifested right up to head level. However, the real issue here is the stress of not being able to express fully, truly, who we are. How can we do this? How can we clear the stagnation so we can raise our resonance and be in touch with universal wisdom?

PART II
ENLIGHTENMENT

Chapter 8

Light, Resonance and Disease: A New Paradigm

What if light actually does control everything? Think about it for a moment. Without light from the sun, there would be no life on Earth. Light is the life-giver and also the healer, within as well as without. Light is important to us on a metaphorical and physical level – winter is associated with darkness and death, while summer is associated with rebirth and life. Living to our potential is also associated with light, inasmuch as it involves maintaining our light within.

HOLDING THE SPECTRUM OF LIGHT

Dr Johanna Budwig, who successfully treated many patients, said that in order to heal our body we had to be able to hold the whole spectrum of light. She didn't just mean the colours in the spectrum – it's much wider than that. If each cell in our vehicle holds its full quota of photons, i.e. as much light as it can, then we're in harmony – in resonance – with life itself. All forms of medicine and healing should have this as their aim.

Some of this is already being recognized. The importance of light in the form of vitamin D3 has been highlighted by medical associations worldwide, particularly for joint and bone issues, while in *The Field*, Lynne McTaggart draws attention to the very strange light emissions when multiple sclerosis (MS) or cancer are present.

Light orchestrates everything within our cells. Remember that it is a prerequisite in attracting oxygen, and when light and oxygen are present in sufficient quantities, transmutation can take place within the cell and there can be a complete electrolyte exchange.

To create and maintain cellular health, we need not only to draw in light but also to understand our place within the cosmos. We live between heaven and Earth and use energy from the Earth (for example, crops) and energy from above (for example, light and oxygen). In past times, we had a greater connection with the soil, as we grew, raised and foraged food in our local environment. We followed the natural rhythms of nature, and food was grown and eaten with respect. This nurtured us, as the Earth was able to donate the maximum amount of electron energy. However, this is not the case in modern life, as genetic modification, fertilizers, processing and food preparation transform our food into less natural forms of nourishment. Its energy is distorted, which in turn affects the donation of electrons to the cells of the body.

We in the West have lost something crucial: our ability to fully experience our connection to the Earth – and also to the sun, to the cosmos. If we look to other traditions, we can see it hasn't always been this way. For example, in the Native American tradition, when someone was ill, a slight dip would be dug for them in the ground and lined with moist grass to create a bed. The Native Americans knew this was the best place to nurse a person back to health because Mother Earth's electron donation was a vital part of the healing process.

Fortunately, a number of modern practitioners are making an enormous difference to people suffering with life-threatening issues by returning to this ancient human understanding. For example, Dr Max Gerson, the German physician who developed the Gerson therapy, has had enormous success treating patients with organically prepared juices and a diet rich in vegetables, among a few other things, which gives them a huge electron donation.

If we live in this way – cultivating our food to hold all the natural energies of the Earth and consuming it with respect – we get back in touch with the light and attract even more positive energies into our cells. For me, this is obvious. Food has an intrinsic connection to the cosmos – it grows under the influence of light and the rhythms of nature – and when it is taken into the body, by donating its full quota of electrons as well as nutrients, it strengthens our own connection with the cosmos, with light, and with universal wisdom.

A CHANCE TO REBALANCE OUR WORLD

We are living on a busy planet on which we rely for survival, so it makes sense to live in harmony with its natural rhythms. They bring us far more than just survival – they bring us balance.

As already mentioned, in Traditional Chinese Medicine each season is responsible for influencing a different organ, and each organ is linked to the expression of a different emotion. Each day we have two-hour periods of energy flowing through the different organs. These are further influenced by the phases of the moon. This means there are natural cycles in which each organ, and the emotion that organ expresses, is focused upon for a certain time in order to keep things moving in the body. So our vehicle is, at all levels, the manifestation of a direct connection between heaven and Earth. We could also say that our body ought to be the manifestation of our soul. The problem is that modern life seems intent on moving us further and further away from our natural connection, and so further away from our potential.

However, it seems to me that one of the greatest rebalancers is happening now – in the Age of Aquarius. The elliptical orbit of our solar system around the star Alcyone takes approximately 26,000 years, which means that at certain times we are much closer to it than at others. In 2012 we entered its photon belt, so for the next 2,100 years we'll be bathed in far more photon energy than at any other period of time since the last Age of Leo. In the past, times of high photon activity have coincided with great leaps forward in human development, and so it seems that during this period we will have an immense opportunity to receive more universal wisdom. We may find that ancient paradigms resurface, such as telepathic ability and other phenomena that we now consider miracles, such as spontaneous healing.

It seems to me that it is vital that we harmonize with the natural processes of life so that we can maximize our receipt of this light and its universal wisdom. But, of course, first we have to be able to encode it into our body in order to understand it.

I believe this cosmic event is happening at a crucial time in human history, as everywhere we see wisdom slipping away – a prime example being the greed and dominance that has left the majority of the planet's inhabitants starving while a minority is overfed and wasteful. But if we get the only thing that we truly own – ourselves – into some sort of shape to take up our position between heaven and Earth, then we'll see a return to the light and be able to resolve the issues we face.

RECEIVERS AND TRANSMITTERS

The Water element of our body is an intrinsic part of changing what has gone so badly wrong, because it maximizes the resonance of the universal wisdom transmitted by light. If we hold and produce as much light as possible, we will be able to transmit that light in a never-ending exchange with the universe.

I really believe that the way we communicate with each other is via light. The first part of this communication is experienced as empathy. We know whether we're comfortable in somebody's presence; we know whether there is resistance or understanding. When we are light beings, there is no friction, because light moves through each cell of the body, meaning there is no discomfort or dis-ease, and very clearly from one person to another.

As a facilitator, my role is to help other people to bring light into their bodies by finding out who they are. With that understanding, their roles become clear.

I think this is what we mean when we use words such as 'enlightened', 'intuition' ('inner tutor') or 'insight', but if we widen our perspective from the small area of ourselves to the large picture of the universe, then these words take on a higher significance: they describe methods of being part of that bigger picture – being a conduit between the Earth and the heavens.

Universal Wisdom

Many people talk of light as bringing in universal consciousness, which in turn brings the ability to receive and transmit love and knowledge. I'd like to suggest that being respectful in the way that we grow, prepare and eat our food is central to that idea. Just as disrespecting the planet has brought untold environmental damage, so taking damaged produce into our body damages us. When we respect the natural world and live as part of it, however, light does bring consciousness, awareness and caring; it's designed to create a beautiful resonance, a healing vibration that moves through us.

We know that all sorts of things can influence our ability to receive and transmit this universal wisdom – thinking acidic thoughts, suffering acidic relationships or jobs, being under stress.... On the other hand, when two people are in resonance, as when healing is taking place, the discharge of bio-photons is measurable. This is extraordinary evidence that people have the ability to transmit and receive light to each other. For me, this is such a natural condition, and an enjoyable one. It is almost as if the body is transmitting joy and love and so creating comfort and healing, just as the sun itself comforts and heals the body.

Flow and Stagnation

When people speak about reaching their full potential, they often mean getting straight A's in exams, expressing their creativity or having an important job, but this is a very limited view of potential – only the social perspective. The bigger picture, the one that is my focus in this book, happens when we manifest our potential within the universe, through holding and radiating the full magnitude of light that is appropriate to us and our make-up.

On the other hand, the biggest dissociation from universal energies happens when we are unable to hold light and live to our potential. That's when we lose track of who we are and enter a state of dis-ease. This coincides with Dr Budwig's views that healing is all about maximizing the full spectrum of light.

Science confirms that each living thing has a resonance, and the idea that every cell of the human body is resonating is so interesting when we consider the fact that we, like the Earth's surface, are mainly water. One can imagine this tune, this resonance, being played on the water and the water holding the message. Of course, that message is constantly changing, as there is freedom and movement within our picture.

When we are dehydrated, however, we contract and harden. Think of arthritis, gallstones, changes in the structure of arteries, changes in the functioning of the brain, heart functioning and lung functioning – in each case, there is an element of stiffening, of hardening, which prevents flow and movement within us.

In our own story, we may know where there is stagnation in our body, where the oxygen is not getting fully into the cells and nurturing us, where the lymph is not draining away. We may not be suffering from named diseases, but this lack of connection creates stagnation, lack of movement, lack of cleansing and a change of conditions within the test tube – pH levels, temperature, etc. – which leads to the sort of hardening that ultimately creates disease.

Due to modern ways of looking after ourselves (or not), this process of hardening, of calcification, can affect the pineal gland (also called the third eye), which is very serious in my view because the pineal gland controls and harmonizes how the right and left hemispheres work together. There's been sufficient research to show how important this function is in our connection with consciousness. Let's look at how we can improve this connection now.

Chapter 9

Connecting Back to Consciousness

Imagine for a moment Adam and Eve living in the Garden of Eden, feasting on fruits and living in harmony with each other, the Earth and the heavens. The theory of evolution tells us that this idyllic pair are unlikely to be our natural ancestors, but whether we accept the scriptures or evolution as our guide, we know that at one time we lived mostly on fruits and raw foods, in small societies and in harmony with our natural surroundings. When we think back to our natural forebears, we'll also know that, despite all the marvellous advances of the 21st century, it is likely that they were more intuitive, more in tune with universal energies and weren't born with a toxic load. And for one good reason: diet and lifestyle.

Diet and lifestyle are vital factors in whether our toxic load increases or decreases throughout our lifetime. But why are we born with that load at all?

If we take a look at the beginning of human evolution, it is fairly obvious that there is a marked difference between our 'natural' diet and the modern diet that most people consume in the West. If we go way back in time, clearly we wouldn't have had heated food, for example. What we would have been eating would have been mostly raw and available with the seasons. Everything we grew would have been close to its natural state and unaffected by fertilizers, pesticides, modern machinery, processing, etc., and what was cultivated would have been appropriate for the soil, climate and the land. We would also have chosen where we wished to live based on the proximity of natural resources.

Some interesting research by Graham Gynn and Tony Wright in their book *Left in the Dark* demonstrates how changes in our nutrition and diet have affected the connection and function of the two hemispheres of the brain – the more logical, analytical and objective left hemisphere and the more intuitive, emotional and subjective right hemisphere. Gynn and Wright suggest that changes in our diet and lifestyle mean that we now operate largely through the left hemisphere, whereas our ancestors would have been more equally brained. For me, this is another indicator of how our diet has moved us away from our more natural way of being and weakened our connection with the Earth and the heavens.

Gynn and Wright hypothesize that early humanity's diet would have mostly consisted of fruit, vegetation, and roots from the plants and the trees, which meant it would have been very similar to what chimpanzees eat now. It is believed the role of the appendix was originally to help us digest the high cellulose content of tree bark and roots. But if we look at that early diet as a source of nutrition, we can see how electron-rich it would be, in the same way that we talk about well-grown blueberries, for example, being electron-rich because they convey the wonderful energy from the Earth.

So, our ancient ancestors would have eaten electron-rich food from the Earth, our richest donor of electrons, and because it wouldn't have been heated, there wouldn't have been any loss of quality or damage to the nutrients. Their diet would also have been extremely rich in bioflavonoids (found in red, yellow, and orange fruits and vegetables), and particularly in beta-carotene, and it is thought that this would have stimulated the pineal gland. Therefore, the body would have naturally produced a high level of melatonin. Nowadays this does not happen and many people believe that melatonin puts you to sleep. This is only true if it is taken in low doses. Melatonin does, however, create a sense of calm and wellbeing. Living and eating in this serene manner, people would have acted in a very different way from today, as the softness and activity of the pineal gland would also have allowed for higher levels of intuition and consciousness.

THE ROLE OF THE BRAIN IN CONSCIOUSNESS

There has been much research into the role of the *corpus callosum*, the connection between the halves of the brain, and the different functions of the right and left hemispheres of the brain. The broader the callosum, the more neural pathways there are between the hemispheres.

Ideally, there should be a good connection between the hemispheres, and they should work harmoniously together. However, we only have to look at Western education and lifestyle to see how dominant the left hemisphere of the brain is and the linear thinking that has developed from there, which has had a very calculating effect on us personally and on the way society has developed. The right hemisphere is much more creative and mellow, and therefore communicating from the right hemisphere strengthens our ability to hear messages from our intuitive mind and connect with the greater consciousness.

In Traditional Chinese Medicine, the brain is placed at the top of the hierarchy of organs and is also the highest aspect of the central nervous system, so it requires the largest number of double-carbon bonds from the diet for development and maintenance. These are found in the four double-carbon bonds of the arachidonic acid (AA) in omega 6 and the six double-carbon bonds of DHA derived from omega 3.

It is estimated that the brain contains 100 billion neuron cells and even more glial cells and so, inevitably, it has the greatest need for light. It stores and communicates information, so it would seem sensible that we should have the hemispheres working well together with a strong connection between the two. It has been theorized that where there is excessive left-hemisphere dominance, there is a more masculine dominance. By this I'm not talking about the differences between men and women, but a more masculine way of thinking, which results in acting in a way that is less conscious and having less conscience about activities. Ideally, the hemispheres should be balanced so that neither is dominant.

If we consider further the function, balance and connection of the brain's hemispheres, we can see how the functioning of the right hemisphere is vital in terms of our connection to higher consciousness, universal wisdom and, particularly, our ability to store that wisdom. Therefore, the more we look after the brain through our diet, the more expansive our wisdom, awareness and way of being are going to be. So many people feel that if they are able to be in touch with a higher aspect of themselves at least some of the time, they are able to be in a creative and peaceful place more often – and this is one of the aspects of meditation.

Throughout the book so far we have looked at hardening. First, in the tubercular picture, we have seen the inability to keep calcium in the right place. Second, we know that when things harden, they become denser and less able to move easily, so hardening lowers the vibration, the resonance, of cells. Third, our generational blueprint, which has come down the line from the individual and collective lifestyle of our ancestors, means that we start out with a toxic load and that parts of the body may be affected by this hardening, including the brain. Finally, the level of hardening that is taking place in the pineal gland means that we are less able to contact our higher consciousness and reach a state of harmony. All of these aspects are affected by how we're feeding ourselves, and receiving the full quota of electrons from our food is vital in maximizing our potential to receive and transmit light.

BORON: THE MISSING INGREDIENT

One of the important ingredients missing from many people's diets is boron, because it needs to be in the soil so it can be taken up by the food; and some soils do not have an adequate supply, or a supply in a form that can be utilized by plants. We know that a lack of boron will create a hardening picture such as arthritis, and it is interesting to note that the lowest levels of arthritis/rheumatism in the world are found in Israel, where they have the highest levels of boron in the soil.

Boron works very much like magnesium by making sure that calcium stays in the correct place. Research published by biochemist Walter Last shows that boron is particularly important for the endocrine system, which produces the hormones that regulate the body's activity, and the parathyroid glands, which are involved in calcium metabolism. If we're short of boron, the parathyroid glands produce a lot of their hormone (parathyroid hormone) in order to find calcium and move it to where it is required. In other words, if we're lacking in boron and magnesium and in addition have a strong tubercular picture, the parathyroid gland will produce an excessive amount of parathyroid hormone and start to take calcium from the bones.

Very importantly, boron also regulates and maintains the softness and flexibility of the cell membranes and the pineal gland. A lack of boron creates a hardening picture in the pineal gland and throughout the body, and this results in a drop in the resonance that is so vital for our connection to the greater universe.

It's interesting to note that the current time is when Rudolf Steiner said we would be at 'our grossest form in terms of resonance'. From now on our resonance will rise. Our work is to help this process, and our body is an important part of that – it is our instrument, the vehicle we occupy.

RECONNECTING WITH THE OLD WAYS

There is plenty of evidence that having a very fresh electron-rich diet strengthens the immune system, and this vital food is exactly what we need. However, in modern life this is not what's on offer. As a result, our immune system is weakening, and unless we take care, this will be passed on generationally in our blueprint.

We have looked particularly at the tubercular blueprint, but when the immune system starts to weaken, other systems in the body are bound to want to help resolve the situation. It's hardly surprising, therefore, that we're currently seeing huge challenges in the hormonal functioning of the body, because having a weak immune system is bound to throw the rest of the body out of balance. Remember, everything is connected.

Just by looking at the sort of diet that we would have naturally eaten in the past, we can see that it would have really enriched the body's immune and defence systems. Equally, if the soil was in balance and electron rich, our diet wouldn't have had the hardening effect we see today. The soil wouldn't have altered the resonance of the food grown in it.

Today, deterioration of dietary habits and agricultural methods means that many of us are eating in such a way that we're hardening the tissues in our body. It's particularly concerning that we're hardening the pineal gland, as this is damaging our connection to higher consciousness. We're also seeing this hardening being expressed as a hardening of behaviour – we're taking a more left-brained approach and so the level of conscience in our behaviour is diminishing. We're also seeing so much manifestation of dis-ease at the brain level, and this seems to be another indicator of how we have lost touch with both universal wisdom and our own wisdom concerning how to function well. Here again we can see a hardening, a lowering of resonance, a reduction in the connection with consciousness and light. It's so important that we work to return our vehicle to the way it used to function.

In times past, people would have been more closely in touch with the Earth, in particular growing their own food, and so it would have been much richer in electrons. In modern life, our food has often been picked before it's ripe and airfreighted overnight before being packed in plastic ready to be sold in the grocery store or, alternatively, so heavily processed that it no longer resembles its natural form.

Many people, of course, are concerned about where their food comes from, and a few embark on a journey to cultivate their own food, but still the connection with the Earth is not what it was. For example, in the past people would have spent a lot more time with their feet in contact with the Earth. Houses would not have had so many levels of insulation between the Earth and where people slept. In other words, there would have been much higher contact with the electrons of the Earth, which is so important if we want to move through the different dimensions to reach the highest possible state; the base of the pyramid has to be strong or it can't climb to the heavens.

The same is true if we want to obtain the full number of electrons from our diet and lifestyle – we need to include Mother Earth in the picture, because her magnetic core is so important to us. We have to be there in that first dimension in order to move through the other dimensions of raising our vibration and bringing in the fullest amount of light and consciousness possible.

FATS AND OILS

Food preparation methods have also changed over the course of history, in particular with regard to heating food. We didn't originally have fire, so everything eaten would have been in a very vital form, which is why it's important even today that we eat a percentage of our food as fresh and raw as possible.

There are different points of view on what percentage of our diet should be raw and what should be cooked, so it's interesting to see what foods could be harmed by cooking. If we look at fruit, vegetables and grains, there's no way that an appreciable amount of damage is going to take place there – these foods may in some people's eyes be 'de-natured' by cooking, with the vitality not being there, the vibrancy. However, cooking won't bring about any gross damage to the components of those foods.

If, however, we look at any foods containing fats and oils, then we'll see something very different. Fats and oils do undergo a change when heated, depending on the temperature.

We know that fats and oils taken in a healthy state are very important for good liver function, and liver function in most people has in fact diminished over time, and we're seeing hardening in this organ, too. In Eastern medicine, the liver and the gallbladder have Wood as their element and are to do with structure, among many other things. They must remain flexible and not be allowed to become so hard that they become brittle or break, nor so lacking in structure that they blow over in the wind.

Of course, oils have long been used outside the body for anointing. If you visit the temples in Egypt, you can still see the remains of rooms once used for mixing the oils for the celebrations, but now we seem to have lost touch with the higher importance of oils, as indeed we've lost touch with so many things. Of course, a lot of chakra work still goes on using oils, and other therapies, such as aromatherapy, while cold-pressed oils are of immense value in the diet. However, I really want to emphasize how difficult the human body, in particular the liver, finds it to deal with heated fats. Although very few people would choose to go through life without heating food, it's important to be aware of how the different oils should be used in food preparation and how they are affected by heat.

There is no doubt that the more heated fats and oils a person eats, the more their liver will struggle and, depending upon the predispositions that are running in them, the more they will hamper their health. It is true for everyone that the liver is important in the regulation of the body's hydration, and if we want to register as much universal information and wisdom as possible, we need to eat in a way that maximizes its potential.

Of all the ways in which diet has changed since humanity first started eating on this planet, I believe it is the fats/oils component that has had the most challenging effect. Of course, as mentioned earlier, certain oils are hugely supportive for the body, but if they are mistreated, they will undoubtedly challenge the liver, which in turn will cause dehydration and cellular contraction.

INCREASING OUR RESONANCE

The emphasis here is on understanding the changes that have taken place in the body, particularly in the hemispheres of the brain, due to our changing diet, lifestyle and food preparation. Perhaps you might agree that we haven't had the respect we should have had for the different components of the world around us, and this has led to a hardening. By this I mean hardening in every single way: hardening of body and mind.

We can see this in the liver with a hardening of expression, a hardening of vibration, a dampening of resonance — and of course the very thing we should be doing is raising that resonance. Rife and Tesla had amazing results with patients using resonance machines, so we know that what we put into ourselves in terms of our nutrition is important in terms of resonance, of how the vehicle forms itself, how it stores light in the electron clouds and how it therefore connects to the different dimensions and to universal wisdom.

We're also living in a crucial time, as we've discussed, with our solar system having just entered an area of space where there is a huge increase in the photon energy available. In order to take advantage of its resonance, its wisdom, we need to have flexibility and softness at a cellular level. We need to be able to reach through the dimensions and be in touch with as much of that photon energy as we can.

The American author Gregg Braden, among others, tells us that the magnetic field around our planet is weakening dramatically. This happens periodically. However, looking at the bigger picture, this weakening is taking place at the same time as the Earth is speeding up (the Schumann resonance), and we have a huge influx of light/photons/universal wisdom. In this environment, we know that all the molecules on Earth, including our own, will move much more quickly.

So, despite having moved so far from nature's intention, we have an opportunity from the stars to turn our way of being around, to raise our vibration, to lose some of our density and to heighten our resonance. We choose, of course, whether or not to take advantage of it, but we can do our part of the job by ensuring that our diet and lifestyle allow there to be more equal hemisphere brain functioning and that our pineal gland is soft and able to receive this universal consciousness. Therefore, one of the most important things to do is to learn from how humanity used to grow and prepare food, so that our vehicle can receive the maximum benefit from this level of consciousness and overcome some of the hardened behaviour that sadly we see too much of today. We will look at this more closely in the following chapter.

Chapter 10

How to Enlighten Our Mind, Body and Planet

We have so many words for light – 'brilliance', 'luminosity', 'radiance', 'lustre', 'glow' – which imply not only the physical aspects of light but also a state of being, of manifesting potential. When we speak about enlightenment, many people think of spirituality or religion, but it means 'light within', and it seems to me that this is exactly what we should be aiming for in our life. Enlightenment is not so much about spirituality as the consciousness that we *are* the light. It means we can receive and transmit universal wisdom. And I see that for each of us, in our own unique way, our purpose is to receive and transmit light everywhere. Let's look at how the way we nourish ourselves can help us to do this.

THE TREATMENT OF THE EARTH AND SOIL

Many people these days are worried by the fact that food is not being grown or reared as nature intended. As a result, the food we eat is not what it once was.

The story of the Earth is that once the soil was perfect and we grew all we needed in it, and so our health was good, but we became greedy and started tampering with it. The first effect of this denaturalization manifested on our skin, as we started to develop what's called 'the big itch'. We know that the skin is quite a superficial organ, the lowest in the hierarchy in traditional Eastern medicine, and issues manifested there are very unlikely to be life-threatening, but as our vehicle changes, these issues will go deeper.

The tragedy is that we have completely lost our original ability to feel when there is an imbalance in the body. It isn't just that we've been taught to be dependent on a pharmaceutical medical system, it's also that we have lost touch with ourselves even at this physical level. Furthermore, changes in how we treat the soil are leading to unnatural food production, which will be reflected in the body.

In his work on biodynamic growing, a method of organic farming that recognizes the universal energies and their interrelationship with the growing of plants as a self-sustaining system, Rudolf Steiner saw the soil influencing living matter in the same way as Béchamp saw the microzymas influencing the cell. The conditions outside the root system influence the health of the plant just as the microzymas in the cellular fluid influence the health of the cell.

All food should, if it's grown in the correct way, manifest the 'as above, so below' principle, because plants are part of that interconnection between the Earth and the heavens. In this respect, they're no different from humans or animals. What is interesting is that a plant will show when it is out of balance much more quickly than humans or animals.

To bring back balance, I believe we need to go back to understanding how light and soil are vital to our existence. This is what independent environmentalist and futurologist James Lovelock proposed in his 'Gaia hypothesis'. Gaia was the goddess of the Earth in the ancient Greek religion, and Lovelock's theory postulates that the Earth's biosphere is a self-regulating entity with the capacity to keep the planet healthy by controlling the chemical and physical environment. However, if we keep tampering with Gaia's natural rhythms, just like the human female, or the female of any species for that matter, she will not reproduce. There are certainly parts of the planet where we are already seeing the unfortunate results of our meddling with Gaia's plan.

Peter Tompkins and Christopher Bird's thorough research in their book *Secrets of the Soil* clearly indicates the benefits of biodynamic agriculture and tells a wonderful story about how an old man, in the middle of the day, when the sun was at its hottest, played his wind instrument beautifully to give a resonance to his crops. And, in spite of the drought conditions, they grew amazingly well.

By comparison, what is the resonance being put into the Earth by so-called modern farming methods? Fertilizers, pesticides, manipulated seeds and forced growth all set up an appalling resonance.

In Rudolf Steiner's biodynamic approach, the soil is respected and certain methods are used to attract the 'upper energies', the energies of the heavens, into it. In this system, absolutely everything is taken into account. The cycles of the moon, for example, are considered in the planting and harvesting of each type of plant. The grower also considers the needs of each plant and whether it produces roots or leaves or fruits or flowers. This is vital, because all living things have different types of energy, and clearly they are going to be responsive to very different conditions.

This is a beautiful system because it dances with the rhythms of the Earth and the heavens. I spoke earlier about how important it is that we do the same, because our life becomes increasingly painful when we are out of step with these rhythms. The same is true for plants and animals — they're no different.

OUR RESONANCE WITH FOOD

Another concern about our food these days is how distanced we have become from it. The natural way is to live among our land, to grow and cultivate what we eat.

In the past, for example, if we wanted to have an egg for breakfast, we would have gone and collected the eggs laid by our chickens – birds that would have had the freedom to move around their dwelling – and we would have visited those chickens daily, fed them and known them well. In this situation, chicken, egg, person and land are beautifully connected. We should compare this with rushing to an air-conditioned supermarket and grabbing a box of eggs. Who knows where they have come from, how the chickens have been reared, how they've been fed and what the farmer thinks of them? And conditions can vary wildly. For example, some producers play music to their chickens to get a higher egg production while other birds are kept tightly packed in barns or sheds. Yet, however the chickens are treated, the resonance of their eggs is still going to be alien to the people who are going to eat them. And the more closely connected we are to our food, the more we'll be in resonance with it.

How can this be brought about? Growing our own food is one way, though this is not practical for many of us. Another way, as already mentioned, is to bless our food before eating. This act was once common but has died out in Western cultures. Many people shy away from it because of its religious connotations, but blessing food doesn't have to be considered a religious act at all. Think about it for a moment: we rely upon the Earth and the food she provides. Without it, we wouldn't be here. Why not simply acknowledge that and be grateful for it?

There are two things that we can affect in blessing our food. The first is that we can strengthen our connection with it. If we place our palms, which emit our personal energy very strongly, over the food, then we introduce our energy to it before we eat it; it gets a preview of us, if you like. This brings our resonance and that of the food into greater harmony.

Second, it has been found that blessing water reduces its surface tension, so that it moves more smoothly. So, as food is largely made up of water, blessing food enables it to move more freely as well, and this is in line with the purpose of healing: to stop stagnation and create freedom and movement. Water that has been blessed becomes more oxygenated, too, as the levels of hydrogen peroxide increase.

So, in blessing our food, we align our energies with it and increase its movement and oxygen content – and everything starts to configure in a more energetic way.

The moment of blessing is also a moment of acknowledgement, which serves many purposes and is particularly important if we don't have the facility to grow our food around our dwelling, to visit it and, as is mentioned in *Anastasia*, the first book in the Ringing Cedars series by Vladimir Megré, to walk barefoot on the soil around it. Walking barefoot on the soil around the food being produced allows it to harmonize with the energies being emitted via the soles of our feet. It is not dissimilar to the role of the conductor of an orchestra, if you like – bringing the music into harmony, so there's no discord or friction or stress – and has a hugely positive knock-on effect on the electrons that the food donates to our body.

The other aspect of being mindful of how we grow and eat our food is simply about giving respect to the Earth. In indigenous cultures, there are many traditions associated with the Earth, for example, dancing to bring rain. Still practised in some parts of the world, these rituals are just another way of bringing the energy of awareness to the Earth's rhythms and harmonies, because one of the worst things about modern life is our tendency to have fragmented concentration or a high level of distraction. This is particularly detrimental, as it doesn't allow us the time to be centred. When we eat, we should be centred in our being, acknowledge our food, be aware of its sources and so come into resonance with it before putting it to use in our body.

DIET

Diet, of course, is the most controversial aspect of how we eat, and the media is partly to blame for this confusion, as we seem to be assaulted on almost a daily basis by headlines about what we 'should' and 'should not' be eating. Here I want to go through what it is we're expecting to achieve from our nutrition.

To start with, if we look at the body as a test tube and we want our health to improve, then clearly we're set on an experiment of change. Therefore, we need to start by acknowledging the five basic conditions that exist within the test tube, which are:

- hydration

- pH balance

- body temperature

- light

- oxygen

Hydration

We already know that the resonance of stress creates dehydration, which is felt within the body and in turn creates a resonance of stress. So many conditions and issues are actually down to this vicious cycle.

In this situation, we experience the maximum amount of fear possible and so create panic and anxiety within and without. Nothing in the body can function fully, particularly the central nervous system, which is connected to the Water element, so we see autism spectrum disorders, night terrors in children and all sorts of distressed mental states. In this situation, the first thing is to address this fear and maximize the fluid, the water within us, to allow it all to move and relieve the congestion and stagnation.

Water is our medium for hearing messages, holding the resonances from above and below. The colon is our reservoir and registers when we are dehydrated. The lovely expression that people use when they say 'gut feeling' applies here, because the colon is full of nerve receptors and transmitters.

In the East they consider short-grain brown rice to be the food of the colon because if it is grown properly, then soaked and cooked adequately, this grain holds the same ratio of fluid to solid as there is in the human body and as there is of land to water on the planet – 80:20. In addition, if the rice is chewed adequately, it remains alkaline. (*More about the importance of alkaline foods below.*)

Many people suffer with food intolerances and digestive difficulties, which arise because they're so dehydrated in the first instance. As mentioned earlier, we have to be dehydrated in order to create an allergy, because then the mast cells, which are in the colon, start to produce histamines. Food intolerances, too, start with the colon registering dehydration.

When looking at our diet, it is very important that a reservoir of water is held in the colon, rather than in the extracellular tissues or even in the tissues themselves. We don't want waterlogged tissues, but bloating is a common complaint these days, and is usually made worse by the use of medically prescribed diuretics, as these, of course, simply make the electrolyte situation even more imbalanced.

Hydration is always the first place to look when considering diet. What sort of challenging, dehydrating fluids are we using in our diet? Coffee, black teas, sugary drinks, alcohol and hot chocolate will all take fluid away from the body rather than donate it. So, it is never a good idea to introduce these sorts of stressed fluids into the body.

Of course, pure water is the best drink in the world. But the water delivered through our taps may be far from pure. Fluoride, for example, is often added to our water supply. The theory runs that it benefits dental health; however, it also goes into all of the iodine receptors on the cells, blocking them from carrying out their proper function, particularly in the reproductive organs, thyroid and brain. It's worth researching everything that is being added to your water supply.

How much water should we drink in a day? The amount required varies, depending on body size, diet and lifestyle. Two litres (3½ pints) a day are required by some people, while others feel fine drinking less than 1 litre (1¾ pints), as long as they're not drinking dehydrating drinks and are eating enough water-holding food (e.g. fruit and vegetables).

pH Balance

The second condition in the test tube to consider is the pH balance. Stress creates acidity, so clearly our state of mind, the way our food is grown and our lack of harmony with the universe are important factors here. I know of people who have tested the pH of their saliva in the morning and it has been alkaline, but then have had to deal with a stressful situation and have found their pH has 'dropped like a stone'.

You can see from this example how important it is for us to hold the understanding of everything being connected. Everything we do, think and are is a resonance and can be felt in the collective. Do we want that collective to be acidic? Do we want ourselves to be acidic? So, to come back to diet, eating neutral or near-neutral food, such as properly grown millet or short-grain brown rice, is vital, because these grains are less acidic and less challenging to the body. Eating plenty of vegetables, particularly green leafy vegetables, is also important in terms of alkalizing the conditions in the test tube. Other approaches would be making juices, as in the work of Dr Max Gerson, who treated patients with high beta-carotene, high bioflavonoids and carbohydrates and very little in the way of fats and protein. (Apparently Johanna Budwig only introduced oil, which became a part of his therapy, to him quite late in his life.)

The alkalizing aspect is crucial if we think back to the fact that the pH of the body is important in terms of holding calcium in the correct place and of where a person is in the 16 stages of change. More and more we're hearing that chronic disease cannot survive in an alkaline body.

The pH level is a very good indication of what is going on in the body, and it is easy to test, too. Upon waking in the morning, swallow hard to clear the saliva from your tongue, then let it re-accumulate, spit into a very clean spoon and put in a pH strip to test your pH. Of course, this must be done before you brush your teeth or eat or drink anything. After a night's rest and sleep in harmony with the rhythms of the cosmos, your pH should be alkaline – 7–7.5, but not too high. Testing once a week is usually quite a good guide and will tell you whether your diet and lifestyle are serving your body well or not.

Temperature

The third thing we require from our diet is the maintenance of our body temperature. When things have become so stagnant that we can no longer produce inflammation to clear the congestion, our body temperature is often lower than it should be. We lack the energy to clear the issue and so the situation becomes chronic.

In the East, damp, cold conditions are mentioned as a factor in many chronic conditions. It is also worth noting that when the endocrine system is struggling, the body temperature tends to be lowered.

Although I believe that a high percentage of raw food is necessary for health, in this situation we are likely to feel more comfortable if some of our food is cooked. In Ayurvedic medicine most foods are cooked, although there is great diversity in what is considered the best diet, from everything raw to everything cooked. In line with this, I think an individual assessment should always be made. If someone has a cold digestion, for example, it is important to take this into consideration, because maintaining a good body temperature is vital.

Light and Oxygen

If all of these three elements are correct – the hydration, the pH and the temperature – then we'll have no problems creating big electron clouds, trapping the photons of light, attracting oxygen and producing bio-photons within. We'll be able to receive and transmit light.

So, when we're thinking about our nutrition, these are the things we should be assessing. We need to think, *what is it we want to achieve?*

MORE ABOUT FATS AND OILS

We've gone through a phase in the alternative health world of people drowning themselves in essential fatty acids in the name of good health, but what I have observed is that before the coeliac situation (gluten intolerance) arises, the liver cannot handle fats correctly, which means it also cannot metabolize the most important fats and oils.

If we look at modern ways of eating, we have the extremes of, on the one hand, processed and fast food, which is generally laden with all kinds of heated fats, and on the other, a raw food diet, where people eat masses of avocados, seeds, nuts, olive oil, flax oil, almond milk, etc. However, what is becoming evident to me about *both* these paths is that we are totally overloading ourselves with fats and oils and our liver simply cannot cope. Although the liver has much more trouble dealing with heated fats (including those we consider safe to heat), even too many so-called good fats can overload the liver.

If we think about heated fats, the bottom line really is that the body can't handle them. So they should be used very consciously. Remember that the liver is responsible for hydration and the kidneys are the filter, so fats and oils do affect the hydration of the body. This is confirmed by my experience, as I often find that when people cut back quite severely on their intake of fats and oils (in particular, heated fats), they start to hydrate and lose their sensitivity to certain foods.

I think it's very easy to blame modern food – too much of this, too much of that – and some of it is not nutritious, but I do think it's important that we also look at the reasons why there has been an incredible increase in intolerance to grains, such as wheat and oats, which used to be a more unusual occurrence. If we understand that it is our inability to handle fats that precedes the coeliac picture, it makes so much sense why other food intolerances are becoming more widespread, too. For example, I have found the same picture in the so-called healthy diets of people eating a diet high in nuts and seeds, because these are concentrated foods and simply overload the liver. If we are dehydrated, due to the liver not handling fats adequately, then intolerances will follow.

Initially, as we know, we wouldn't have cooked our food, so fats and oils wouldn't have been heated. However, looking through the ages, we see all sorts of fats and oils coming into our diet, grown in different temperatures and varying degrees of light and climate, and often heated; and what we're seeing in the West today is that so many of our foods now contain fats and oils, causing our intake of these to increase dramatically compared to our intake of fruit and vegetables.

The human body did not evolve eating this type of diet, so it's not surprising that health has never been worse in the Western world. What a number of cardiologists and specialists in type-2 diabetes have found is that fats and oils are not being broken down effectively by the liver. The effect of this is that these unbroken-down fats and oils clog the lymphatic system, slowing down its movement. The lymph then drains into the blood, causing thickening of the blood and clumping of the blood cells. The unbroken-down fats also lead to coating of the walls of the blood vessels.

CREATING POSITIVE CHANGES WITHIN

In my experience, one of the most transformational changes we can make in our diet is to reduce our intake of heated fats and refined oils, particularly those drawn from seeds or nuts. By making this simple change, we are able to increase the body's hydration and liver function, our spontaneous planning, our moods and our feeling of wellbeing, as all these improvements go hand in hand with improving the body's vital Water element.

Furthermore, if we remove the excess of heated fats from our diet, we can ensure that the fats and oils we do need will reach the correct place in the body – the central nervous system in the case of DHA and the endocrine system in the case of EPA.

In addition to reducing our fats and oils, reducing protein in the diet will leave space for more energy foods – unrefined carbohydrates such as fruit and vegetables.

This can be tackled in a variety of ways. In *Left in the Dark*, Gynn and Wright discuss the benefits of an all-fruit diet, which is a high raw carbohydrate diet, while the work of Dr John McDougall also indicates the benefits of a high-plant carbohydrate diet but includes more cooked foods. Then we also have the work of Dr Douglas Graham, who is a raw food advocate and created the 80/10/10 diet, which again focuses on the percentage of a day's food that should be drawn from fats and protein. All of these approaches may work well and there are any number of different nutritional approaches we can take, but the bottom line is that a diet high in fruit and vegetables, with some raw foods and a little fat (in the form of cold-pressed oils) and protein will mean we are able to hold the maximum fluid in the colon and create full hydration within the body.

You might be surprised to learn that animal produce triggers quite a large insulin response in the body. Again, it is fats, whether they are derived from animals, plants, seeds or nuts, and our inability to handle them in large quantities that is the real problem. The message here is, rather than looking at the deficiencies of our diet, we should aim to understand our body's ability to handle and absorb fats and oil and then proceed with caution when using them. We need to use the essential fats and oils efficiently.

MAGNESIUM, IODINE AND BORON – ESSENTIAL COMPONENTS

Finally, there are three essential minerals that I believe are vital in enabling us to reach our full potential and maximize the use of light within the body. They are magnesium, iodine and boron.

First, our aim should be to have plentiful supplies of magnesium in order to put the calcium in the correct place and to create soothing. However, I was reading some older books recently that mentioned that when fats are too abundant, they have the effect of binding magnesium, and this is not good in terms of that hardening picture in the body. This is another example where we may think our diet is on the right track and contains a plentiful source of this important mineral, but it is undermined by another element of our diet – the fats and oils.

Iodine is another mineral that I'm passionate about including in the diet. Although most people believe that it is important for thyroid function, it is also vital for brain function, the blood–brain barrier and for the reproductive organs, as it keeps the oestrogens in balance. This last factor is particularly relevant in modern life because so many oestrogens have been introduced into our environment via plastics, hormonal contraceptives, even food, and these non-natural forms of oestrogen confuse the body's receptors and can create hormonal havoc.

In addition, when iodine is in short supply but we have the addition of fluoride, there is a further difficulty. Because fluoride, like iodine, is a halogen that is very active, it can rush into the iodine receptors and create problems.

I discussed the importance of boron earlier in the book, but would like to mention it again here. This book is all about how we can soften and raise our vibration, and boron has a very important place in this transformation. Boron drives magnesium, which drives calcium into the correct place. Good supplies of boron are vital to ensure that we don't have calcium misplacement, as in the TB taint. The reason for this, you will remember, is that if our boron levels are depleted, then the parathyroids will keep producing parathyroid hormone in order to find calcium and restore it to its proper place, and this encourages the withdrawal of calcium from the bones. Boron is also very important in the softening of the pineal gland, the third eye, in the functioning of the left and right brain hemisphere and in our connection with consciousness.

In summary, I don't think there's ever been greater confusion and contention about the way we should be eating. But I am completely sure of one fact: most modern diets include too many fats and oils, particularly heated fats, and our liver has no way of knowing how to cope with this abundance. Left unchecked, these unbroken-down oils and fats negatively affect the body's hydration and have the potential to create endless food sensitivities and most of all fear and anxiety due to disruption of the Water element. They have the potential to eventually cut us off from the light.

Chapter 11

A New Way to Health

Throughout this book we've looked at how, over the years, the changes in our diet, our lifestyle and our connection with the Earth have affected the health of our body and our ability to receive, hold and transmit light and manifest our true potential. Let's recap this here, before going on to look at a new way of moving forward.

STRESS

The first and most critical point is to understand that disease is created by the resonance of stress. It seems to me that there are two main sources of stress that affect the body: stress created by unresolved emotions and stress created by our lifestyle. Of whatever kind, stress causes dehydration, which disrupts the body's fluids and so makes it more difficult for us to dance to the rhythms of the universe. This gives rise to further stress and so we find ourselves in a vicious cycle: stress creating dehydration and dehydration creating stress.

So often this situation arises due to an unsuitable diet. All food has a resonance, and we need to make it easier for the body to hear – easier for the two to connect and be in harmony. However, it seems to me that more people now suffer with food intolerances, such as intolerances to wheat and gluten. I can only surmise that this is due to how we are producing our food – that its resonance has been distorted, and therefore it is more challenging for the body and creates greater absorption problems. To give you just one example, 40 years ago Crohn's disease could be resolved by simply removing wheat from the diet, but now we have to remove wheat and gluten in order to achieve the same resolution, and maybe all grains temporarily.

There are many different diets, but due to our individual predispositions, our diet has to be the one that suits our own body, the one that creates the least stress for us. It's helpful to look at our ancestral line here.

DEHYDRATION

We know that to function fully, the brain should be 80 per cent water and the rest of the body 70 per cent, so it's easy to see that if our fluids diminish in any way then the flow of our entire being will be affected. Without sufficient hydration, the body is unable to move in a free-flowing way on all levels of its existence.

Each day the body needs to remove and eliminate acidic matter produced by the metabolic processes. This cleansing is vital in maintaining the pH of the blood and the rest of the body tissues. When there is dehydration, this cycle is disrupted, as the lack of fluids prevents the smooth movement of cleansing, elimination and nurturing.

The liver controls hydration, and for most people the issue that causes stress and then manifests as dehydration is consumption of heated fats, which are prevalent in the modern diet: e.g. baked goods, processed foods, spreads and margarines, etc. Most people do have an awareness of good and bad fats, and of course we all need good fats (the DHA, EPA and AA) in our diet, but the key is moderation, otherwise those good fats just won't get through. A drizzle of cold-pressed oil, a little butter or coconut oil, one portion of oily fish a week is enough, not the extremes we see today, where people are consuming bags of nuts and seeds in the name of good health. 'Storage' foods such as seeds and nuts are dormant, so they should be soaked before eating, and just a few each day will provide health benefits without overloading the liver.

CONGESTION AND STAGNATION

When the body's cleansing process becomes inefficient, the liver is normally the first place to show congestion, due to its role as the main internal organ of elimination. If the liver begins to struggle with its role of detoxifying the blood, the level of toxicity within the blood begins to rise.

If this situation is left unsupported, the blood system will struggle to receive and cleanse the lymph effectively. The lymph will therefore become thicker as its own level of toxicity begins to rise and will start to stagnate. Often the throat is the first place where we notice this, as it manifests as dryness, a sore throat, swollen glands or even just tenderness in the throat area – also swollen lymph glands in the neck, under the arms, in the breast tissue, etc.

Next, the movement of the blood slows, so we have poor circulation, with sticky and congested blood.

If this situation is also left unattended, it will affect the cell exchange and cause cellular congestion and stagnation. This situation is the precursor to an acute episode, as the body tries to heal and rebalance.

In my experience, no matter which stage of the elimination process appears to be struggling, it is the liver that needs supporting first. When you support the liver with techniques (see Appendix), you improve its efficiency during the detoxification process. Once the liver is coping again, you can return to the original area of congestion and apply the appropriate techniques to create movement. Then the liver will usually require further support to ensure that it can deal with the extra toxicity that is released.

What's important to remember is that congestion and stagnation are part of the hardening process and require careful management in order to resolve the situation and get things flowing again.

INFLAMMATION

Stress, dehydration, congestion and stagnation clearly need to be resolved, but this often doesn't happen. The body knows that this situation is not a healthy one, so it takes action and creates inflammation, e.g. a sore throat, eczema, a bladder infection or another mild issue.

Now we notice the issue because it is uncomfortable, so we take action. But instead of resolving the stress, we respond to the inflammation by suppressing it, perhaps with painkillers, antibiotics, creams or other pharmaceutical products. Left to its own devices, however, the inflammatory process will usually resolve the toxicity in the tissues and morbid matter, particularly initially in the lymphatic system and lymph nodes.

Most acute illnesses have inflammatory processes, and sadly these are the ones that Western medicine suppresses with drugs or creams until they don't appear again. We see this particularly in the tonsils, which will throw up inflammation many times and have it suppressed many times, until, perhaps, they are surgically removed altogether. Meanwhile the congestion in the lymphatic system goes unresolved.

Common types of inflammation that occur before the end of puberty include ear, nose and throat infections, allergies to dust, pollen, etc., eczema, psoriasis and IBS. If any of these are suppressed often enough and the person has strong predispositions, the body loses the energy to throw up inflammation. and the issue moves deeper.

At this stage of the disease process, we have been given valuable information by the body. Inflammation is alerting us that there is stress in our mind or lifestyle that needs to be fixed in some way. In the meantime, the inflammation does need careful nursing for the release of the dehydration, stagnation and stress, but once resolved, the best course of action is to review what is causing the stress and then work on removing it and supporting the body more, perhaps by changing our diet, using a particular technique (see *Appendix*), finding more opportunities to relax, improving our life–work balance, etc.

What this situation does *not* need is anything 'anti' – anti-inflammatories, antivirals, antibiotics, anti-histamines – because they will not resolve the issue. Suppressing inflammation without resolution will increase the congestion and stagnation, causing dehydration and further stress on the body, which means it will be even more predisposed to this inflammatory condition.

ENCAPSULATION AND ISOLATION

If the inflammation isn't resolved by reducing the previous stages, then the toxic tissues and morbid matter continue to fester, and the body enters a process of encapsulation and isolation. This creates a much more challenging situation and, with the heavy use of prescription medications and lifestyle choices, it is one that is being seen more frequently in the West.

Here, we know that the cleansing process has been interrupted, so we have a displacement of minerals in the cell, which Gerson spoke about in his observations of patients, and this tends to result in the positioning of sodium and calcium in the wrong place. This creates hardening in the tissue, and therefore by definition, less flow, and we know that healing is facilitated by freedom and movement on all levels.

Furthermore, we know that when a cell is completely stress free and operating properly, it will create its energy, ATP, from 80 per cent oxygen and 20 per cent glucose. However, when stress continues, inflammation is continually suppressed and toxic tissues and morbid matter all maintained, then the cell will begin to move into energy-sparing mode until finally the ATP will be produced almost anaerobically, from 80 per cent glucose and only 20 per cent oxygen. At this point the cell becomes foetal-like in behaviour and starts to reproduce itself in its desperation to maintain the ATP output.

Any breakdown of cell operation means a weaker connection to the resonance of wisdom from above – oxygen and light – and less ability to attract life-giving electrons from below, from our food and from the soil. And so our connection with Earth and heaven is diminished.

By this stage, there will be huge internal stress on the body, and the vicious cycle of stress causing dehydration and dehydration causing further stress will be in operation. For example, I have met people who have experienced a lot of stress from their busy lifestyles and then been diagnosed with high blood pressure later in life, which is not surprising because the kidneys control the Water element, and this shows up as high blood pressure. However, the prescribed blood pressure pills cause indigestion, acid reflux and disruption to the stomach. Further prescription medicines are then given to disguise the inflammation in the oesophagus or stomach. However, the issue is unresolved and so the inflamed tissue changes; it becomes isolated and encapsulated as its ability to attract light and oxygen substantially decreases. In turn, this lack of light and oxygen affects transmutation, calcium enters the cell and the process of hardening begins.

In this situation, silica can be helpful, because, as Rudolph Steiner suggested, many people are deficient in this trace element, and it is required for the health of all the connective tissues – skin, blood vessels, cartilage, bone, teeth, tendons and hair. Silica has the ability to create appropriate structures, which is not surprising because it is one of the Earth's main components, and it is found in barley, oat stems and many other vegetables, as well as nettles and horsetail.

EVERYTHING IS CONNECTED

With disease, the most important aspect to remember is that everything is connected in the body. Stress is easily transferred and inflammation needs to be resolved rather than suppressed or obliterated.

The whole theme of interconnection is shown clearly in the dental connection. Each tooth corresponds, via a meridian, to a particular part of the body, and so often inflammation in the root canal and the jaw can affect the corresponding part, either creating or indicating a deeper problem within the body.

CASE STUDY

I knew a man who was having an issue with his liver that couldn't be explained by his doctor and didn't respond to treatment. However, it was noted by his dentist that he had a tooth that hadn't erupted. When the tooth was surgically removed, it proved to be completely decayed; furthermore, it was lying on the liver meridian. Here we see the inflammation of the tooth carrying the message of the meridian.

This is something that I often see in practice – this connection between the root canals of the teeth and inflammation in other parts of the body, particularly the thyroid or thymus, which may have presented the first symptom in an illness.

CASE STUDY

A woman in her mid-30s consulted me because she was suffering from an extreme expression of anorexia. In her case history there were a number of throat infections in childhood, and then in puberty she started to diet, although just to stay slim, nothing extreme. It was an extraordinary case because she had only been diagnosed with extreme anorexia two years earlier, when she had been hospitalized due to a coma. So what had happened to switch her from keeping slim and being an active mother who had successfully breastfed without any postnatal depression to being anorexic?

Delving deeper into her story, I discovered that the anorexia had manifested after a course of antidepressants, but that the depression was the result of two admissions to the hospital with acute pneumonia, where she was treated with intravenous antibiotics. Here was the trigger. For this situation to manifest, she obviously had a certain level of imbalance and predisposition, but it was the suppression of the acute inflammation that pushed the issue to a fully blown central nervous system condition of anorexia. The lungs were her vulnerability, and when the inflammation was suppressed, the issue moved to the brain – this was the missing link and the cause of the anorexia.

EASING STRESS THROUGH DIET

Our predispositions and lifestyle are the reason, I believe, why we end up with a particular health scenario. Predisposition is, of course, vital, but there will usually be a dietary or lifestyle trigger that starts the disease process. As I said earlier, the stress of diet can be enormous, because all food carries a resonance. I want to look briefly here at how we can use our diet to support our body and resolve stress. Everyone is unique and therefore the dietary recommendations for each person will also be unique, but there are some general guidelines.

It may seem logical to add fluids in order to rehydrate the body, but not all liquids are hydrating. Caffeinated drinks, including black tea and coffee, alcohol, sweetened soft drinks and drinks containing colourings and aspartame, actually have a diuretic effect, effectively increasing dehydration. Instead, I recommend drinking between 2 and 2.5 litres (3½ to 4 pints) of water at body temperature each day, but never more than 1 litre (1¾ pints) in any given hour.

Sugar, aspartame and other artificial sweeteners should be avoided, likewise table salt, though sea or Himalayan salt may be used instead.

What we put into the body has to create very little stress and in fact support the body. It is important to remember that the resonance of food can be changed depending upon how the food is grown, harvested and prepared for eating. An animal from a factory farm will have a very different resonance from one that has been allowed to roam free. All sorts of foods have also had an array of chemicals added, such as pesticides, fungicides and preservatives, which will also add their particular resonance to the food. So we should aim, as far as possible, to eat food in its natural state, avoiding all artificial additives, colourings and preservatives. This way we can be sure that the body will recognize the food and be able to process it with the minimum of effort, thus creating extra energy that can be focused on healing.

Certain foods will cause the body particular stress and be difficult for it to absorb easily. Disaccharides and grains, in particular, are implicated in all sorts of disruptions in the central nervous system, for example, autism and schizophrenia. The most challenging of the grains is wheat, followed by rye and then oats and barley. These four glutinous grains are all challenging and can present a problem to anyone who is overly acidic or dehydrated. At the lower end of the scale are short-grain brown rice and millet. Both of these are considered to be gluten-free grains. Depending upon our story, we might need to remove wheat, gluten or even initially all grains from our diet. Quinoa (which is a seed rather than a grain) can provide an alternative.

Dairy products are also challenging because in the West most are pasteurized and much of it is also homogenized. Both of these processes change a natural product into one that is both unnatural and of little nutritional value. Furthermore, by the age of two we lose the enzymes required to break down and utilize milk, because that is normally the end of the breastfeeding phase.

Yoghurt has been partially digested by the bacteria present within it and so presents much less of a challenge. When it is made from a less processed milk such as goat's milk, it is even less challenging.

Cheese can be very challenging because most of it is pasteurized and has had salt added to it in order to harden it. Consuming foods high in sodium presents a strong challenge to anyone who is dehydrated.

Generally, dairy produce, with the exception of yoghurt, butter and ghee, presents too high a challenge for the body and would be best replaced by seed and nut milks. Also, dairy products have a tendency to unbalance the electrolytes and are mucous forming, meaning that they tend to thicken and thus reduce the flow of lymph.

Vegetables should account for at least 60 to 70 per cent of two of the meals during the day, and it is best to eat them in a seasonal way. This means not only looking at which vegetables grow in a particular season but also deciding whether they should be predominantly cooked or raw. If blood sugar is implicated, it is often necessary to concentrate more on leafy vegetables rather than the sweeter root vegetables until the blood sugar remains consistently stable.

Fruit is also best eaten in a seasonal manner, meaning that in a temperate climate fresh fruit would only be consumed during the summer, and during the winter dried fruit would be used.

Proteins can be acid forming, but they are also good stabilizers of blood sugar, so often need to be included in meals, especially for blood sugar stability. Whenever meat and fish are eaten, one can balance out their acid-forming properties by adding plenty of alkalizing leafy green vegetables to the meal. Eggs can be a problem for some people who suffer from asthma, but for most people they are an excellent source of protein and can be eaten every day if desired.

Some people find pulses difficult to digest, but they are made much easier if soaked overnight and even more so if they are left until they just start to sprout (changing the water frequently).

As for fats and oils, heated fats should be kept to a minimum, but if required for cooking, butter, butter ghee, coconut oil and animal fats are the safest to use. Virgin olive oil and other cold-pressed vegetable oils should only be added to food after it has been cooked.

If we help the bowel and liver with a suitable diet and lifestyle, any issues we have can be resolved at an early stage and won't move to more sensitive organs such as the lungs and kidneys and then heart and mind.

In summary, the following recommendations will help reduce stress in the body and resolve any issues:

- Hydrate by drinking plenty of filtered water low in inorganic calcium to avoid and reduce internal stress.

- Support the liver by avoiding heated fats as much as possible.

- Keep other fats to a minimum so that the DHA

and EPA and AA can get through to where they're needed.

- Have enough iodine for all the cells in the body, particularly the brain.

- The body needs light, so vitamin D3 is paramount in ensuring health.

- Include plenty of vegetables in your diet (with a good proportion of raw foods) to maintain an alkaline pH and steady body temperature.

- Gluten and wheat are very stressful for the body, so switch to less challenging grains, e.g. rice and millet; or quinoa, amaranth, chestnut and buckwheat, which are good carbs but not grains.

- Dairy products are also very challenging because they are intended by nature to nourish baby livestock, not humans.

- Understand the complex nature of proteins and choose your sources carefully – aim to use organic, local and free-range foods wherever possible.

- Use the techniques outlined in the Appendix to support the body in eliminating toxins; these techniques are healing and create flow on all levels.

Conclusion

Returning to the Light

If we look back to when we started out on our amazing process of evolving as a species, we will see that our lifestyle and diet would have enabled the two hemispheres of the brain to work harmoniously and equally, while the softness of the pineal gland – the third eye – would have meant that it was fully functioning in a way that is, perhaps, unknown to most modern humans, so that there would have been a fairly constant flow between an individual person and higher consciousness and back again. The same is true of light, too – whether we call it 'the source' or 'the divine' or 'enlightenment', it would have flowed from above to within, and from within to without, expressing the resonance of who we are.

There is no reason why we cannot manifest this in modern times, too. We are living during a very important time in human history, a time when many parts of our story have become diminished, including our health and the health of our planet; and vast polarities are experienced in our society – rich–poor, wasteful–starving, free–oppressed. So, with this in mind, it is vital that we take full responsibility for expressing who we are and living in consciousness of mind and deed. Each of us is a part of the collective resonance, and each of us can make a difference. It is as if we are just a tiny dot, but that dot is connected to the whole puzzle of expression, and if we each manifest our potential in the hugely connected, *beautifully* connected universe, then we will create a very different world here on Earth.

Our body, our vehicle, is the physical manifestation of our resonance. But is it the physical manifestation of our original resonance – the resonance of divinity? Maybe not, because there are Eastern teachers who say that our body is the physical manifestation of our karma. Although controversial, to me this makes total sense, as my background is in homoeopathy and energy therapies. To explain this in more detail, in five-element acupuncture, practitioners talk of the causative factor and are looking for the first element that went out of balance in the person's life. Equally, they are looking for congenital predispositions or congenital causative factors that have been brought into the person through the generations, and are also looking at the ancestral energy brought in through the kidneys, through the Water element, which I think is very relevant in terms of this element being the medium for holding those vital messages of our potential. In homoeopathy we talk about the miasms, the energetic blueprint brought through and manifested in a baby. So often now people speak of someone having a 'quadruple tubercular miasm', meaning that all four grandparents have experienced that situation of miasmic overload, and it is being passed on as an energetic imprint to the following generations.

So, we are carrying these predispositions, but nevertheless we do have the opportunity to be fully connected to the cosmos and return to the original state of health our ancestors enjoyed. As soon as stress enters our story, however, whether it comes through eating food that's unbalanced, thinking thoughts that aren't quite right, performing actions that don't accord with our conscience or having a generally unhealthy lifestyle, then dehydration will set in and we will be heading towards a state of stagnation and hardening rather than flowing as we should, and manifesting our full potential as a human being.

Nevertheless, through understanding and acknowledging this process, we have the perfect opportunity to diagnose our vulnerabilities and undertake the work required to move things back to a more fluid, connected state. This is particularly true if we think of this hardening picture in relation to an organ such as the pineal gland, with its role in harmonizing the hemispheres of the brain. By reversing this process we can regain our connection with the universe.

The loss of this connection is perhaps the most damaging aspect of this hardening picture in modern life, but it is easy to see why it has happened. As children we are taught in a most disconnected way, and then we live in a majorly disconnected way – disconnected from the Earth, from the heavens, from each other. You only have to look at most modern families to see this lack of connection. Jobs, too, are often very disconnected from the ability of the people doing them. What is the driving force here – happiness and fulfilment or money and necessity?

In the same way, we have lost our awareness of living in tune with the planet. Our understanding of the forces that create our food has been replaced by anonymous foods from anonymous places, and we've exchanged rain dances for nipping down to the supermarket. But at what cost?

This level of disconnection permeates modern life, and so it is no wonder that so many of us suffer with depression, anxiety disorders and mental distress or feel dislocated and unable to fit in or find purpose and meaning in life. These states of mind are a symptom of modern life and due not only to our lack of individual consciousness but also to our lack of social consciousness, which is further manifested in the wars, the exploitation and the great inequality currently seen in humankind.

But now we're living in an extraordinary time where we're being given a chance to resolve these issues and shake off our karmic inheritance. Here we are, living in the photon belt of Alcyone and able to access these photons of light where universal wisdom is held. With that amount of information available to us over the next 2,000 years, we're bound to be more connected, more in tune with the universe, than we have been in recent times. Equally, at the moment we have the Schumann resonance, the pulse of the Earth, vibrating so strongly and quickly that it is shaking everything up. This is an enormous opportunity.

How do we start? With ourselves. There is only one thing that we have the right to change, and that is ourselves – our body, our mind and the manifestation of our consciousness. Changing anything else is exerting force from outside, and exerting force is not the gentle movement and flow we are looking for. Moreover, as everything is connected, our body, our vehicle, is a very obvious place to start to bring harmony and peace into the world.

If we understand where we've come from, how the imbalances have been imprinted gradually – probably over many generations – and are here now in our body, we can then take things forward in a new way. We have a great opportunity for change, a great opportunity to receive universal wisdom and a great opportunity to shine, to bring in and manifest light. We can create a world in which there will be no place for deception or lies or depression, but a true understanding of the connections we have to each other, to the Earth and to the heavens, to the ancestral sound. Let's start now.

Appendix

The Techniques

In this Appendix, I want to introduce you to a range of simple yet powerful techniques, which I presented in *Cellular Awakening* but have included in this book, too, because they form the most important part of my practice; and I have, over the years, found them to be uniquely effective.

It requires a fair amount of energy for the body to generate the necessary movement for cleansing, balancing and purification. Usually this energy comes from the body itself, but if we are ill or overtired, our ability to bring forth extra energy is often impaired. This is where techniques can be extremely useful.

With techniques, we want to create movement in stagnant areas, or we want to bring heat to cold areas, or just want to bring more energy to a particular area where energy is very low. Using careful selection and a holistic understanding, we can employ these techniques to provide that much-needed energy to start creating movement. Even more importantly, the following techniques can be utilized to ensure that any stagnation or toxicity, which starts being released, continues to move all the way out of the body.

The techniques vary greatly, as each one targets a particular area of the body or supports a particular process. However, they all have a common goal: to help the body achieve balance in areas where it is struggling. They enable us to access any part of the body and offer it some assistance.

When employing techniques, it is important to be sympathetic to what you are asking the body to do. It is all too easy, with over-enthusiasm, to make too many changes without considering what the consequences of those changes might be. When the body is not healthy, it is basically under-functioning, and therefore all of its systems are in some way impaired. To start shifting excessive amounts of stagnation or toxicity and to expect these impaired systems to cope with this extra workload on their own is unrealistic. Patience is required if you want to bring your body back to health. You must endeavour to release a manageable amount of toxicity when you begin changing your diet and lifestyle. Also, it is important to ensure that the toxicity moves through all of the levels of detoxification and out of the body. This can be managed with the aid of techniques. Once you have released the initial toxicity from the body, and it is in a slightly improved state of health, you can then re-evaluate the situation and perhaps employ further treatment and managed elimination. This is where listening to your body becomes vitally important. It needs to be gradually returned to balance rather than overloaded with mobilized toxicity.

With this in mind, let us look again at the process of detoxification and how we can support it.

DETOXIFICATION

How Does the Body Detoxify?

The body has a set process for detoxifying, and all of the stages of that process need to be functioning well for health to be returned and maintained.

Remember that in a healthy body, toxins are removed automatically using the following route:

1. Toxicity is released at a cellular level into the lymphatic system (some toxins leave the lymph and are released from the body via the skin and lungs).

2. The toxic lymph then drains into the blood (some of the toxins leave the blood and are released from the body via the skin and lungs).

3. The blood passes through the liver and the liver filters out the toxins.

4. The liver excretes the toxic bile into the bowel.

5. From the bowel, the toxins are excreted from the body.

What Happens If Detoxification Is Impaired?

In a body where detoxification is impaired, toxicity can get blocked at any of the above stages. For example, the toxicity released from the cell can stagnate in the lymph. If this toxicity is allowed to stagnate for a long time, the body will begin to show signs of illness such as swollen glands or a sore throat. These symptoms arise as the body attempts to move the stagnation onwards. It might even create a fever to thin and move the lymph. In this example, you can offer the lymphatic system some assistance by employing techniques. If you can help to move this stagnation from the lymph, the body can then attempt to finish the process and excrete the toxins.

To take another example, if the liver becomes overloaded with toxicity, the toxins will back up in the blood, and if the bowel is sluggish, the whole system of detoxification grinds to a halt. In order for the liver to release its toxic bile freely into the bowel, the bowel needs to be evacuating effectively. You can begin to see just how important it is for our health and wellbeing that this primary route of elimination is open and working freely. If this is not occurring, there are some techniques in this chapter to rectify the situation.

In reality, in the first example, it would not be possible to have stagnation in only the lymphatic system. There would also have to be significant stagnation within the liver and the blood to cause the kind of symptoms described.

Due to its important role as the main internal organ of elimination, the liver is normally the first place to show congestion when the body is trying to heal and rebalance. If it begins to struggle with its role of detoxifying the blood, the level of toxicity within the blood begins to rise. If this situation is left unsupported, the blood system will struggle to receive and cleanse the lymph effectively. The lymph will therefore become thicker as its own level of toxicity begins to rise. If this situation is also left unattended, the cell will begin to have trouble releasing into the lymph system and this will cause cellular congestion.

In my experience, no matter which stage of the elimination process appears to be struggling, it is the liver that always needs supporting first. When you support the liver with techniques, you improve its efficiency during the detoxification process. Once the liver is coping, then you can return to the original area of congestion and apply the appropriate techniques to create movement. Then the liver will usually require further support to ensure that it can deal with the extra toxicity as it is released.

The real art in using these techniques is in keeping the speed of elimination at an even rate throughout all of the systems, from the cell to the outside of the body. If this is achieved, the detoxification and healing process will be comfortable and continually empowering. It will also ensure that no areas of the body are left unsupported. However, this requires you to take full responsibility for yourself and how you feel. For me, techniques are about empowering individuals to take personal responsibility for their healing and to give them the tools to make health a reality. So let us explore these techniques.

SKIN BRUSHING

The skin is the largest organ of elimination; this makes it a very important organ to work on when supporting the body's natural healing process. The purpose of skin brushing is to first remove the scurf layer (the uppermost layer of skin), which holds a certain amount of acidity and toxicity. To brush this layer away makes a whole new surface area available through which to excrete toxins. Brushing the skin also promotes movement within the lymphatic system and thus helps to prevent stagnation and the thickening of the lymph. Thickening of the lymph often happens when the body performs a cleansing process. This is because when the body releases toxicity, the lymphatic system has to work hard to move the toxicity to the blood, but without the benefit of a pump (unlike the circulatory system with the heart).

Skin brushing on a daily basis can benefit everyone because it can help to move both toxins and mucous through the body to be released. Excess toxicity and mucous in the lymphatic system can easily stagnate if not kept freely moving.

If you are constipated, it is best to avoid skin brushing, as it will create more material needing to be excreted via the bowel. In this case it would be best to support the bowel first with other techniques.

To skin brush, you need a moderately stiff brush. A back brush with a handle is ideal, as it makes reaching all of the body very simple. You can purchase brushes especially designed for skin brushing from many health stores and internet health sites. Keep the brush just for skin brushing. It is best not to wet it, as it will lose its effectiveness.

Skin brushing is applied to dry skin to ensure the scurf layer is easily removed. It is appropriate to do it in the morning or the evening. The movement of the brushing is always towards the heart, as this is where the lymph enters the bloodstream. Do not apply skin brushing to varicose veins, painful rashes or open wounds.

Instructions

1. Start brushing with gentle but brisk strokes on the top of the right foot and work your way up the entire right leg (front and back). The brush strokes should be felt but should not be painful.

2. Brush on top of the left foot and work your way up the entire left leg.

3. Brush the front and then the back torso upwards towards the heart.

4. Brush the right hand and work your way up the entire right arm, up to the shoulder.

5. Brush the left hand and work your way up the entire left arm, up to the shoulder.

6. Brush from the neck down to the heart, first on the back and then on the front torso. Do not brush the face or head.

Skin brushing can have a similar effect to doing exercise. It can make you feel more refreshed and alert, due to the movement it creates within your body. It can help take away that tired feeling that some people experience first thing in the morning or after work in the evening. It is particularly helpful in cases of ME when a person is feeling more tired in the morning than before they went to bed, due to the night-time stagnation of their system. These people are usually too ill to exercise, and so skin brushing can greatly help to get things moving.

HOT AND COLD SHOWERING

This technique helps to create movement within the circulatory system, which in turn has a knock-on effect on the lymphatic system. The lymphatic system travels around the body in very close proximity to the blood circulatory system, and so anything that speeds up circulation will also help to create movement within the lymph.

Hot and cold showering magnifies the effect of skin brushing, so a beautiful sequence is to do skin brushing first and to follow this by hot and cold showering.

When the body is subjected to heat (e.g. a hot shower), the blood moves in greater volume to the surface of the body (i.e. the skin). This enables the body to lose heat more readily to ensure an even temperature is maintained within the body's vital organs. When the blood moves to the surface, the lymph will follow.

When you subject the body to cold (e.g. a cold shower), the blood moves in greater volume to the inner body. This enables the body to keep the inner vital organs warm and ensure that a balanced temperature is maintained at all times. When the blood moves to the inner body, once again the lymph will follow.

This means that by simply warming and then cooling the body, we can increase the activity within the circulatory system. In doing this we also increase movement within the lymphatic system.

Hot and cold showers can be taken at any time of the day, but are especially useful first thing in the morning (after skin brushing). This can help the body to begin shifting any stagnation that has arisen overnight. The skin brushing starts to create movement within the lymph, and a hot and cold shower afterwards can capitalize on this and provide increased power for accelerated movement.

NOTE *It is very important that this technique is not applied in such a way as to bring stress or shock to the body. Some people are unable to cope with vast differences in temperature, especially those who are pregnant or suffer from a heart condition or high blood pressure. Set the temperatures at levels that suit you and then slowly increase the differential over time.*

Instructions

1. Have a wash in a normal warm shower.

2. Turn the temperature gauge to cool or cold (depending on your level of tolerance), and remain in the shower until your body feels cool or cold.

3. Turn the gauge back to warm or hot (again depending on your level of tolerance), and remain in the shower until your body feels warm again.

4. Repeat this process twice (i.e. three times in total), and be sure to finish with a cool or cold shower.

Hot and cold showers have a similar effect to skin brushing but normally to a greater degree. They can make you feel refreshed and alert, as if you have just kick-started your system into action. They can be particularly useful in situations where people experience sore throats and where the lymph glands in the neck begin to swell. If this situation is left unsupported, the body will want to create a fever to heat the body, thus thinning the lymph and accelerating movement.

If a person is very low in body energy, hot and cold showering can be invaluable, as it is able to supply energy to the body to get the system started and begin to move the stagnation.

HOT AND COLD TUBBING

This technique is a deeper and more extreme version of hot and cold showering, and therefore has the potential to create a great deal of change within a person, especially in situations of extreme stagnation. When the body is heated up to create a temperature, it has the following effects:

- It helps to melt the cholesterol layer surrounding the cell that hinders the elimination of toxins from the cell in a situation of dehydration alert. Once this layer has been melted, the toxins are able to leave the cell and enter the lymphatic system for removal.

- It heats up the lymphatic system, making the lymph thinner and more fluid. This allows the lymphatic system to cope better with the increased workload created by the cellular release of toxicity and to move the toxins further out of the system ready for excretion.

- It makes the blood move to the surface of the body, and this, as in the previous technique, promotes further movement within the lymphatic system to aid proper elimination.

- It opens the pores, enabling further elimination through the skin itself.

When the body is cooled down, it has the following effects:

- The body produces latent heat from deep within to warm itself and counteract the cold conditions.

- This movement of heat from within to without produces increased energy for elimination.

As this technique is so powerful at bringing about deep change within a person, it needs to be used with care and at the correct time. It is a wonderful way to promote elimination, but you must be sure that in doing it you do not overload the system, causing a new set of problems. It is not wise to use this technique without having already made significant changes to help open up the routes of elimination.

This technique is invaluable in cases where the cells are overly protected by cholesterol and have thus lost their ability to fully release toxins into the lymphatic system. It is also most useful in situations where the body temperature is very low due to high levels of toxicity and dehydration, and when the body is showing signs of viral activity. It can also be used if you are not showing any great symptoms but simply want to help your body flush out toxins. It is a wonderful way to cleanse the cells and help the body reach a state where it can complete its detoxification cycles with ease.

This technique is ideally used before bed so that you can sleep through the night and allow the body to process the released toxicity. It is ideal to use if your body has lost its ability to naturally produce a fever.

NOTE *Do not use this technique where there is a risk of haemorrhaging, high blood pressure or in pregnancy. Also avoid just after eating, as this may cause nausea.*

To apply this technique you need:

- a normal household bath

- a body thermometer

- a small towel

- a hot water bottle (to help warm the body at the end of the technique)

- another person to help oversee the technique and to provide support if required

Instructions

1. Lie in a bath at a normal bath temperature.

2. Apply a cool wet towel to your head to ensure that it does not get too hot.

3. Add hot water to the bath at a gradual rate to begin raising the body temperature. Continue with this process until either the temperature has reached 38.9°C (102°F) or, prior to achieving that temperature, you feel that you are as hot as you are able to tolerate. Be sure to monitor your body temperature throughout by placing the thermometer in your mouth, and to keep your head cool.

NOTE *It is not safe to raise the body temperature to more than 38.9°C [102°F] unless you are in a supervised clinical environment.*

4. When you feel that you have had enough time in the hot water (every person's limits are different) or you have managed to maintain your body temperature at 38.9°C (102°F) for 20 minutes, start to add cold water to the bath. This will gradually start to bring the body temperature down.

5. Take the bath temperature down to a cold but manageable level and lie in it until your body is feeling cold.

6. Once this state has been reached, get out of the bath. Then you can either dry yourself by rubbing yourself with your bare hands to create friction or you can dry yourself with a towel. Then go to bed with a hot water bottle. Once in bed your body will start to produce heat in order to return its temperature to normal. Keep checking your temperature with the thermometer to ensure that it is increasing at a steady rate. Warm socks and a hat can be used if required.

Hot and cold tubbing can produce differing effects depending upon the individual. Often people feel very relaxed and tired afterwards, but some can feel invigorated and ready for action. Occasionally a temporary feeling of nausea (due to bile release) or light-headedness (due to a reduction in blood pressure) can occur.

Douglas Lewis performed some of the most exciting work done using this technique. As mentioned earlier, he observed that the HIV virus was only able to sustain itself in low body temperatures and reasoned that if you heated the body up to provide an artificial fever, changes would occur that would make it non-viable for the virus. He found that the symptoms were gradually cured.

HOT TUB, COLD WRAP

This technique is the same as the previous technique, but a cold damp wrap replaces the cold tubbing section. This works in the same way as cold tubbing, but with the following advantages:

- It encourages the movement of latent heat from a deeper level within the body. This is because the body has not only to return its own temperature to normal, but also to work much harder in order to dry and warm the wrap to ensure the correct body temperature is maintained.

- It moves latent heat for a longer period of time due to the longer exposure to the cold and wet conditions. This in turn creates movement of toxicity at a deeper level within the body.

NOTE *As with the previous technique, do not use this technique where there is high blood pressure, pregnancy or a risk of haemorrhaging. Also avoid just after eating, as this may cause nausea.*

To apply this technique you need:

- a normal household bath

- a body thermometer

- a small towel

- a cotton sheet (half the size of a single sheet or a single sheet folded in two)

- a polythene sheet (to protect the bed), a hot water bottle (to help warm the body at the end of the technique), another person to help oversee the technique and to provide support if required.

Instructions

1. Place the polythene sheet on your bed to protect it from the cold damp wrap.

2. Prepare the wrap by soaking a sheet in cold water, wringing it out and placing it in the freezer for the duration of the hot tubbing stage.

3. Lie in a bath at a normal bath temperature.

4. Apply a cool wet towel to your head to ensure that it does not get too hot.

5. Add hot water to the bath at a gradual rate to begin raising the body temperature. Continue with this process until either the temperature has reached 38.9°C (102°F) or, prior to achieving that temperature, you feel that you are as hot as you are able to tolerate. Be sure to monitor your body temperature throughout by placing the thermometer in your mouth, and to keep your head cool.

   NOTE *It is not safe to raise the body temperature to more than 38.9°C [102°F] unless you are in a supervised clinical environment.*

6. When you feel that you have had enough time in the hot water (every person's limits are different) or you have managed to maintain your body temperature

at 38.9°C (102°F) for 20 minutes, carefully get out of the bath.

7. Wrap yourself in the cold wrap (ideally from the neck to the feet, although usually from under the arms down to the thighs is more comfortable), then go to bed with a hot water bottle. Once in bed your body will start to mobilize latent heat in order to return its temperature to normal. Keep checking your temperature with the thermometer to ensure that it is increasing at a steady rate. Warm socks and hats can be used if required.

8. This technique has the same effect as a full-blown fever. It moves toxicity from a painful inflamed area out through the skin via the lymphatic system without challenging other vital organs, and so can be useful in cases such as grumbling appendix or adhesions. It is interesting to note that the wrapping material can be discoloured by the end of the technique due to the toxic release through the skin.

SITZ BATH

This technique is very similar to the hot and cold showering but allows for more precise targeting of the pelvic region of the body. Like the hot and cold showering, it is aimed at creating movement within the circulatory system and thus within the lymphatic system.

Sitz baths bring both movement and energy to the reproductive system, bladder and bowel. In addition, the muscles relax when heated and contract when cooled, which can improve the muscle tone of these organs. Sitz baths are invaluable when you wish to stimulate movement within the pelvic organs. It is especially useful in muscular weakness, e.g. bladder weakness.

NOTE Do not apply this technique if there is any risk of haemorrhaging, or during pregnancy.

To apply this technique you will need:

- a normal household bath
- a small tub (such as a baby's bath).

NOTE You can use two small tubs if there is no bath available.

Instructions

1. Fill the bath with hot water up to a level of about 12.5 cm (5 in).

2. Fill the small tub with cold water up to a level of about 12.5 cm (5 in).

3. Sit in the hot water with your knees up for several minutes while continually splashing water over your lower torso.

4. Change baths and sit in the cold water with your knees up for several minutes while continually splashing water over your lower torso.

5. Repeat this process three or four times and be sure to finish on cold.

6. Dry yourself with a towel, or with your hands if you want to create further movement.

7. After applying this technique, the bowels or bladder often need evacuating, due to the movement created.

This technique is very useful in cases of prolapsed organs, as the alternating hot and cold temperatures exercise the muscles by relaxing and contracting them. This exercise helps to tone the muscles and thereby keep the organs in the correct position. It also helps with a hardening prostate, as the hot and cold temperatures stimulate movement within the blood and lymph and help to shift the stagnation that is contributing to the hardening.

EPSOM SALTS BATH

This technique focuses on the skin as a route of elimination. The skin is the largest organ of elimination, and therefore can be an invaluable route through which to release toxicity, especially if the other organs of elimination are struggling. Epsom salts (magnesium sulphate) have the effect of drawing toxicity and acidity (especially uric acid) towards themselves. As a result, bathing in a high solution of Epsom salts draws toxicity from within the body out through the skin and into the solution.

It is interesting to note that Epsom salts were traditionally used to bring boils to a head, and this clearly demonstrates this attraction between them and toxicity. The bath itself heats the body up, which opens up the cell membranes to release toxicity. It also thins the lymph, enabling it to help with the extra workload, and it encourages the blood to come to the surface of the skin. When Epsom salts and a hot bath are combined, they can produce a great deal of movement within the body to help remove toxicity.

Epsom salts have another very useful benefit because they are a sulphate. Within our bodies we need to convert the sulphur that we take in through our food into sulphate. In certain conditions, particularly in cases of autism, this conversion does not happen.

Magnesium in the sulphate form is very soothing, so simply adding Epsom salts to a bath can have a remarkably soothing effect on body and mind. It is especially helpful with children and young people with autism or behavioural problems.

This technique is beneficial for anyone who is undertaking a detoxification programme or has problems completing their daily elimination process. It is especially useful in soothing aching muscles or joints and so can be employed after heavy exertion or with conditions such as arthritis. Please note that it should not be applied if there is risk of haemorrhaging, high blood pressure or during pregnancy or menstruation.

Taking an Epsom salts bath once a week for three out of four weeks is a great way to ensure that the body keeps moving and releasing toxicity during the darker and more stagnant time of winter.

To apply this technique you will need:

- a normal household bath
- I kg (2.2 lb) of commercial Epsom salts (available from farm suppliers and garden centres)

Instructions

1. Pour the Epsom salts into an empty bath.

2. Run the bathwater and agitate the salts to maximize the dissolving process. The bath should be warm to hot, depending on the intensity required. If running a hot bath, remember to wrap your head in a cool wet cloth.

3. Lie in the bath for up to 20 minutes (everyone's tolerance level is different, so be guided by how you feel). Do not use soap or add any other substance to the bathwater, as this can diminish the drawing-out process.

4. Once you have reached your limit (or 20 minutes have passed), you can do any of the following:

- Add cold water to the bath to bring the temperature down and encourage the body to mobilize latent heat.

- Take a cold shower to encourage the body to mobilize latent heat.

- Quickly dry yourself and go to bed and continue sweating to encourage lymph movement and the release of toxins through the skin.

NOTE *If using an Epsom salts bath with children, the bath temperature should only be warm, and after the bath the child should be dried normally. This is a great technique to use with children before bedtime. Do not use where there is high blood pressure or a heart condition.*

Upon completion of this technique, some people can feel a little weak and tired and so need to rest. After a good night's sleep, when the body has completed the induced elimination, people often feel very clear and refreshed.

FOOTBATHS AND WRAPS

Footbaths have a less dramatic effect on the body than the full tubbing techniques but are able to concentrate their activity on a major area of elimination, namely the soles of the feet. This gentler effect can be very useful for people who need to take their healing process slowly at the beginning. Rather than subjecting the whole body to full tubbing, which creates a lot of change, you can start things moving gently by employing various types of footbath. This technique is also useful if you do not have a bath or cannot get into a bath due to a disability. It can easily be performed while sitting in a comfortable armchair.

Mustard Footbath

As with the tubbing techniques, a mustard footbath aims to create an artificial temperature within the body. This temperature thins the body fluids, creates movement and causes the body to sweat and detoxify through the skin. It is ideal if you want to start creating movement slowly within the body. As the effects are mild and the changes slow, it is an easy way to release toxins out of the body without overstressing it. This is an ideal technique to perform before bedtime.

To apply this technique you will need:

- a footbath (or a bowl the size of a washing-up bowl)

- English mustard powder

- a blanket

Instructions

1. Place a rounded dessertspoonful of English mustard powder into the footbath.

2. Add hot water to the bowl to a temperature that is comfortable.

3. Place your feet in the bowl to raise your temperature and begin the detoxification process.

4. If possible, place a blanket over your entire body, including the head, as this will help to induce an artificial fever for cleansing.

5. Remain in the footbath for 15–20 minutes (or less if you feel that you have had enough time).

6. Once you have completed your time in the footbath, dry your feet and go straight to bed to allow the elimination process to continue.

Epsom Salts Footbath

This technique is a milder and gentler version of the Epsom salts bath. It encourages the drawing of toxicity out through the skin and is also very soothing. Like the mustard bath, it is ideal before bedtime.

To apply this technique you will need:

- a footbath
- commercial Epsom salts
- a blanket

Instructions

1. Place 4 tablespoons of commercial Epsom salts into the footbath.

2. Add hot water to the bowl to a temperature that is comfortable.

3. Place your feet in the bowl to raise your temperature and begin the detoxification process.

4. If possible, place a blanket over your entire body, including the head, as this will help to induce an artificial fever for cleansing.

5. Remain in the footbath for 15–20 minutes (or less if you feel that you have had enough time).

6. Once you have completed your time in the footbath, dry your feet and go straight to bed to allow the elimination process to continue.

COLD FOOT WRAP

This technique draws the blood supply down to the feet as the body seeks to warm them and restore the temperature balance within the body. As a result, the rest of the body loses heat (especially the head).

This technique is very useful for two conditions. First, it is helpful in cases of fever if you wish to bring down the temperature of the head. Secondly, it is great if you suffer from an overactive mind before sleep. Many people do suffer from this, especially if their daily routine is stressful. This technique draws the blood away from the head and gives the brain the space to relax and induce a restful sleep.

To apply this technique you will need:

- one pair of cotton socks
- one pair of woollen socks

Instructions

1. Soak the cotton socks in cold water and wring them out until they are damp.

2. Place them in the freezer for 5–10 minutes.

3. Take them out of the freezer and put them on your feet.

4. Put the warm woollen socks over the top of them.

5. Go to bed and rest.

CASTOR OIL PACKING

Castor oil has been known since ancient times for its healing properties. Known as the *Palma Christi*, or Palm of Christ, it was used extensively by Edgar Cayce in his work with patients.

It is difficult to find a complete explanation as to why castor oil has such healing properties, but its results have been comprehensively documented. It is known to emit white light, which, like ordinary daylight, contains all the wavelengths of the visible spectrum at equal intensity. This white light penetrates the cell, giving it the energy to promote movement and thereby lessening the level of stagnation. In addition, it is known that the human cell produces its own measurable light in the form of bio-photons from within its DNA helix. It is my feeling that castor oil packing promotes the creation of this cellular light, which the body can then use as energy for healing.

Castor oil packing is probably the ultimate technique for bringing energy to an area of the body that is struggling to shift stagnation. It is such a versatile technique that it benefits all situations, with the following exceptions: high blood pressure, during pregnancy or menstruation, or if there is a risk of haemorrhaging.

When applying castor oil packing, there is a constant rule that should be applied in all situations: *wherever a problem area may be, you should always pack the liver first.*

This ensures that this main route of elimination is open and ready to receive toxicity when it is released from the troubled area. Once the liver has been opened, you can apply a castor oil pack to the problem area to release the stagnation.

To apply this technique you will need:

- a piece of unbleached brushed cotton or woollen material measuring 67 × 30 cm (27 × 12 in)

- a bottle of castor oil (organic)

- a roll of cling film or similar material

- a hot water bottle

Instructions

1. Fold the unbleached cotton into double or treble thickness.

2. Place it on a flat, washable surface.

3. Pour on enough castor oil to cover it well but not so much that it starts to drip.

4. Place the oily cloth over the liver area.

5. Wrap cling film over the cloth and around your body to keep it in place.

6. Put on some old clothing in case of any leakages.

7. Relax and place a warm hot water bottle over the liver area and leave for one hour (in situations of extreme stagnation, a longer duration may be required).

8. After you have packed the liver, you may repeat the process by packing any specific area of discomfort.

Castor oil packing is a powerful technique that will always create movement in the body. It should be applied with caution to anyone who suffers from high blood pressure. If in doubt, apply the pack initially for only ten minutes in order to assess how you feel. Furthermore, because of the movement this technique creates, it may be useful to follow it with a further technique (e.g. an enema) in order to maintain the movement of toxicity through and out of the body.

On completion of this technique (and often during it), there is usually a feeling of deep relaxation. Pains and spasms are normally soothed and subside.

The frequency of castor oil packing will depend upon the situation, but I recommend that even in extreme cases this technique should not be implemented more than five days per week.

Areas that respond particularly well to packing are the liver, colon, lungs (on the front and the back) and reproductive areas, but any area of inflammation or toxicity will respond. Furthermore, the endocrine system, with its connection to light, also responds well to castor oil packing, so applying this technique to an area such as the thyroid can be most beneficial.

When castor oil packing is used after surgery, it can prevent the formation of hard scar tissue and adhesions (the pack should be applied as soon as possible after the surgery). It likewise helps to relieve the discomfort of old scar tissue.

In cases such as bronchitis, castor oil packing to the lungs stimulates the movement of lymph and the draining of the congested lung tissue. Once again this should only be applied after first packing the liver.

ENEMAS

An enema is a very ancient technique in the world of healing and is an extremely powerful tool for bringing about swift change in both mind and body. The colon presents a very efficient route through which to bring therapeutic substances into the body because there is a direct connection between it and the liver. Whenever any substance, including all foods and liquids, enters the body, before it can be used it has to be marked as 'friendly' so that the immune system does not attack it; and it is within the liver that this labelling occurs, so the more quickly a substance arrives at the liver, the more quickly it can be used by the body. There is a large vein, called the portal vein, which connects the colon to the liver. Much of the absorption of nutrients from our food takes place in the small intestine and the colon or large intestine. The portal vein carries these nutrients to the liver, so anything that enters the colon via an enema will be similarly absorbed and transported via the portal vein directly to the liver. This makes enemas some of the most potentially potent and swift ways to bring about a change in the body biochemistry. The specific action of an enema will depend upon the therapeutic effect of the substance added to it.

Another function of the colon is eliminating waste products from the body. Waste matter is moved through the colon by a series of circular and spiralling muscle movements. Fibre is vitally important in the diet so that the muscles surrounding the colon wall have something to work with. A diet of highly refined, over-processed foods that are low in fibre can lead to a weakening of this movement. This can mean that food does not pass efficiently through the system and can become stuck in the small pockets along the colon and impacted along the colon wall. This material then starts to ferment, making the colon very toxic. These toxins are then reabsorbed by the body, effectively overwhelming the liver with toxicity that it then has to try to store somewhere within the body. This is called 'auto-intoxication' and is the body poisoning itself with toxicity because it has no effective route of elimination open to it. Constipation is often the first sign of this problem. Similarly, dehydration is registered in the colon, and if someone is very dry, problems with constipation and the re-absorption of toxicity can arise.

Regular daily bowel movements are a sign of good health, and enemas can greatly help to keep a sluggish bowel clean and the body hydrated while a purification and healing process is unfolding. Whenever there is a substantial release of toxins into the blood and lymph, an enema is the most effective way to carry those toxins out of the body. However, once health and balance are achieved, enemas should only be used as part of a health maintenance programme (e.g. once a week or once a month).

Many people are resistant to trying enemas, but they can be an extremely powerful way of speeding up the healing process and bringing both a physical and mental improvement.

NOTE *Do not use enemas if there is a prolapsed organ in the pelvic area or if haemorrhoids are a problem.*

How to Do an Enema

To apply this technique you will need:

- a gravity-feed enema bag or bucket and a 1-litre (2-pint) jug

- the fluid to be used for the enema (this will vary depending upon the type of enema)

- a pillow

- something to protect the floor from liquid (towel or plastic sheet)

- lubrication (castor oil is very good)

- a hook upon which to hang the enema bag

- a clock for timing

Instructions

1. Prepare the enema fluid (as described in the specific enema types below).

2. Hang the enema bag/bucket on the hook so that the bottom of it is about 1 metre (3 feet) above the position you will lie in.

3. Check that the tap is closed, then pour the enema fluid into the bag/bucket.

4. Release the air from the tube by allowing a small amount of liquid to run through.

5. Lubricate your anal area.

6. Prepare the floor area with protective material and then lie down on your back with your knees up or, if preferred, lie on your right side. The pillow can be used to support your head.

7. Insert the nozzle into your anus. (Some enema bags come with two different size nozzles. Use the smaller nozzle, as the larger one is designed for vaginal douching.)

8. Open the tap and allow the fluid to gently enter the rectal cavity. Massage your abdomen while the fluid is entering.

9. When all the fluid has entered, close the tap and remove the nozzle from your anus.

10. Hold the fluid for the specified time (as described in the specific enema types below). If you feel any discomfort, such as wind pains, massage your abdomen until it subsides.

11. On completion, move to the toilet to evacuate the enema.

Notes

- A water enema may be advisable before any other enema to clear the bowel in preparation.

- If you have difficulty holding an enema, try reducing the fluid quantity and/or the holding time.

- Enemas often become easier if you are submerged in a bath of warm water, as the abdominal muscles are able to relax.

- It is not advisable to do enemas when hungry.

- It is not advisable to do stimulating enemas (e.g. coffee enemas) before bed.

Water Enema

If you have never experienced an enema before, a water enema is perhaps the best kind to start with. It introduces approximately 1 litre (1¾ pints) of water into the colon, which has a number of beneficial effects. It creates movement within the colon, encouraging it to release stored faeces. It also stimulates the reflex points within the colon. These points connect the colon to all other parts of the body. Stimulating these reflexes has the effect of releasing stagnation in areas of the body connected to these reflexes. Movement within the colon also stimulates movement and release of mucous from within the lymphatic system. Furthermore, some of the water held in the colon will be absorbed into the body, quickly helping to improve overall hydration.

Water enemas can be applied wherever the bowel is showing signs of constipation or where the lymphatic system is showing signs of stagnation (e.g. a cold or 'flu). They can also be useful when help is required to maintain the movement and release of toxicity during a cleansing programme or if you wish to improve the body hydration quickly (e.g. after a long-haul flight).

After completing a water enema, people feel light and refreshed. Sometimes light-headedness can occur. If so, rest is required. Occasionally, if the body is very dehydrated, the colon will retain all of the water so that no evacuation takes place.

Instructions

1. Prepare 1 litre (1¾ pints) of filtered water at body temperature. (It should be at body temperature because if it is too warm it will sedate the bowel, and if it is too cool it will stimulate it.)

2. Follow the instructions numbered 2–11 in 'How to Do an Enema' (see *pages 190–91*).

3. Hold the water for 10–15 minutes.

Triple-Water Enema

To apply three water enemas in sequence has a greatly increased effect. This technique is ideal at the onset of a cold, 'flu, sore throat or sinus congestion to bring extra stimulation to the lymphatic system. This extra stimulation will often ensure that the body does not need to create a full-blown fever in order to thin the lymph.

Often after completing this technique a person can feel rather drained and tired, so it is good to do it at the end of the day, as then you have the space to go to bed and rest.

If you suffer from a blocked head and sinuses at the onset of winter, it is sometimes useful to implement a triple-water enema three times within 36 hours. This can often relieve congestion that might otherwise persist until the spring.

Instructions

1. Prepare 1 litre (1¾ pints) of filtered water at body temperature.

2. Follow the instructions numbers 2–9 in 'How to Do an Enema' (*pages 190–91*).

3. Once all the water is in, massage the colon and then expel.

4. Repeat this process twice more (i.e. a total of three times).

5. The final water enema can be held for 10–15 minutes if desired.

Aloe Vera Enema

The water part of this enema does the same as described in the water enema technique. Aloe vera is moisturizing and soothing, so adding it to a water enema has an anti-inflammatory effect upon the mucosa of the colon. This makes it ideally suited to aiding any inflammatory conditions within the digestive system.

Often on completion of this technique a person feels calm and fresh, and it can have a very positive, softening effect upon the skin.

Instructions

1. Prepare 1 litre (1 ¾ pints) of filtered water at body temperature.

2. Add between 1 and 10 tablespoons of aloe vera juice, depending upon the intensity required.

3. Follow the instructions numbered 2–11 in 'How to Do an Enema' (see pages 190–91).

4. Hold for 15 minutes, massaging the colon throughout.

Coffee Enema

A coffee enema is perhaps the most powerful detox tool for the liver. It works in a unique way and is extremely useful once a purification programme is under way. The pharmacologically active part of the coffee is absorbed into the haemorrhoidal vein within the colon and is transported through the portal system directly to the liver. When the coffee arrives, it causes the liver to contract and squeeze its toxic bile out through the common bile duct into the duodenum and then out through the rest of the digestive tract. This contraction has a clearing effect upon the liver and leaves it in a much better state to continue with its detoxification role.

Because coffee enemas accelerate the liver's ability to detoxify, they reduce the risk of overload resulting in auto-intoxication. They can also be implemented in the case of an acute liver problem (e.g. migraines) to decongest the liver and bring about a quick solution.

Upon completion of this technique, people can feel remarkably different in both mind and body. They often feel clear-headed, and any aches and pains are reduced. They also feel less toxic, and so have clearer vision and clearer thoughts and are in a better frame of mind. If there was any nausea before, this often disappears.

Coffee enemas can be useful if, for instance, you have done castor oil packing the night before and wish to continue the movement of released toxicity. They have been used by the Gerson cancer therapy for decades due to their ability to help the body remove toxicity when tumours are breaking down.

You do need to be *very careful* with this technique, as it is one of the easiest to misunderstand. Coffee enemas do cause some loss of electrolytes (calcium, magnesium and potassium), which can cause stress in some cases. If overused or used in the wrong situation, they can bring about stress in the kidneys and adrenals due to this diuresis. As they have such profound effects, I always recommend that they be used only within a supervised programme.

Instructions

1. Place 1 rounded tablespoon of coarse ground organic coffee into a non-aluminium saucepan. (This measure can be reduced for a gentler effect.)

2. Pour on 0.25 litres (½ pint) of filtered water and bring to the boil.

3. Turn the heat down and simmer for 15 minutes, leaving uncovered.

4. Sieve into a 1-litre (2-pints) jug.

5. Make up to the required volume (0.5–1 litre/1–2 pints) with filtered water. Be sure to test that the fluid is at body temperature.

6. Follow the instructions numbered 2–11 in 'How to Do an Enema' (see pages 190–91).

7. Hold for 15–20 minutes.

Choline Bitartrate Enema

It is not clear exactly how choline bitartrate (a B vitamin) acts when taken in the form of an enema, but in practice it seems to increase the efficiency of the liver. This technique is especially useful where nausea is present. It can also be used as an alternative when a coffee enema should not be used (e.g. in a person who is very dehydrated, where the loss of electrolytes could cause problems). Choline bitartrate is gentler on the kidneys and the adrenals than a coffee enema, so it is useful when these areas need nurturing.

Upon completing this technique, people often feel very clear. It can be useful in cases of recurring nephritis to effectively relieve intense nausea without stressing the kidneys and adrenals.

Instructions

1. Dissolve between 1 level teaspoon and 2 rounded teaspoons (depending on the intensity required) of choline bitartrate into a water enema.

2. Follow the instructions numbered 2–11 in 'How to Do an Enema' (see *pages 190–91*).

3. Hold for 15–20 minutes.

Chamomile Enema

Chamomile tea is a gentle sedative and when added to a water enema is absorbed via the haemorrhoidal vein (as with a coffee enema). It travels via the portal system to the liver and has a calming effect upon it and the rest of the body (i.e. the opposite effect to a coffee enema), so it is used to bring calmness to the liver, body and mind.

Often on completion of this technique people feel very calm, especially within the digestive system. It is very useful to have this enema in the evening before going to bed, as it aids restful sleep.

Instructions

1. Put a rounded dessertspoon of organic chamomile flower heads into a teapot and pour boiling water over them.

2. Leave to infuse for 20–30 minutes.

3. Sieve into a 1-litre (2-pint) jug.

4. Make up to 0.5–1 litre (1–2 pints) with filtered water. Be sure to test that the fluid is at body temperature.

5. Follow the instructions numbered 2–11 in 'How to Do an Enema' (*see pages 190–91*).

6. Hold for 15–30 minutes.

Magnesium Enema

Magnesium is a muscle relaxant and has a generally soothing effect upon the body and mind. This makes a magnesium enema useful in situations where the muscles have gone into spasm (e.g. acute back pain), at the onset of a migraine if the early symptoms are neck and shoulder tension, and to relieve cramping at the onset of menstruation. It is also useful if there is muscle pain following rigorous exercise.

Upon completion of this technique, people often experience a feeling of calm throughout their body. It is very common for any pains or spasms to disappear.

Instructions

1. Dissolve 1–3 capsules of magnesium citrate (each capsule delivering 100mg of elemental magnesium) in a cup by pouring on hot water and stirring well. Total dissolving is not possible, so there will be a powder residue on the top of the water.

2. Pour the magnesium solution into a 1-litre (2-pint) jug and make up to 0.5–1 litre (1–2 pints) with filtered water. Be sure to test that the fluid is at body temperature.

3. Follow the instructions numbered 2–11 in 'How to Do an Enema' (*pages 190–91*).

4. Hold for 15–30 minutes.

Flaxseed Tea Enema

This is an incredibly soothing enema that is useful for any kind of inflammatory bowel illness such as colitis or Crohn's disease. It is also wonderful for helping to bring hydration to the colon to relieve fear and anxiety and to help to stabilize blood sugar.

To make flaxseed tea:

1. Place 2 tablespoons of flaxseeds (sometimes called 'linseeds') in a large non-aluminium pan.

2. Add 1 litre (1¾ pints) of water and bring to the boil, then immediately take off the heat and cover. Let the mixture stand for 12 hours or overnight.

3. Return the pan to the heat and gently simmer with the lid off for 1 hour.

4. Immediately sieve the tea and discard the seeds. The thick liquid can be stored in the fridge once cooled if it is not being used immediately.

Instructions

1. Mix the flaxseed tea with warm water, bringing the mixture to body temperature and to a consistency that makes it easy to pass through an enema tube.

2. Follow the instructions numbered 2–11 in 'How to Do an Enema' (pages 190–91).

3. Hold for 15–20 minutes.

Flaxseed Oil Enema

Flaxseed oil enemas promote a great deal of photon and electron activity within the body. This technique can be useful at the start of a healing programme to bring more light and electrons into the body. Dr Johanna Budwig would give this enema as her first prescription. It can be used in situations where people are unable to take oil orally due to digestive difficulties or where they are unable to utilize oils (e.g. in people with ME). It is also useful at times of high energy (e.g. at equinoxes) to maximize their effects.

Upon completion of this technique, people often feel an incredible sense of calmness and connectedness. It is very powerful and is usually only performed occasionally, e.g. once a month or once a year.

Instructions

1. Warm a bottle (250–500ml/9–17 fl.oz) of organic flaxseed oil to body temperature by placing it into a jug of warm water.

2. Follow the instructions numbered 2–11 in 'How to Do an Enema' (see pages 190–91).

3. Hold for 60 minutes.

4. Follow the flaxseed oil enema with a water enema to clear the colon of oil.

5. Pour hot soapy water through the enema bag afterwards to clean out any oil residue.

Flaxseed Oil Implant (Mini Enema)

A flaxseed oil implant is similar to the previous technique but acts over a longer period of time. Like the flaxseed oil enema, it can be useful where people cannot take oils orally due to digestive difficulties or cannot break down oils effectively, or at times of natural high energy (e.g. at equinoxes).

Upon completion of this technique, and after a good night's sleep, people often feel very calm, as if the whole nervous system has benefited.

To apply this technique you will need:

- an implant pipette
- 15–60ml (0.5–2 fl.oz) of organic flaxseed oil

Instructions

1. Warm the required amount of flaxseed oil to body temperature by placing the bottle of oil into a jug of warm water.

2. When the oil is warm, draw it up into the pipette.

3. Lubricate your anal area.

4. Insert the nozzle and squeeze the bulb of the pipette so that it pushes the oil into the rectal area. Be sure to keep the bulb compressed constantly until all of the oil has entered and the nozzle has been removed.

5. Ideally, hold overnight.

CLYSMATICS

Clysmatics were developed by one of Sweden's original naturopaths, Birger Ledin, and have been used safely in homes, clinics and hospitals throughout Sweden for over 70 years. The system is medically approved in Sweden and is easily used. It fits into the toilet so that the whole technique is performed while sitting on the toilet. It does not weaken the natural defecation reflexes, and because the liquid is fed into you under only the pressure of gravity, it is much gentler than a colonic (see *the next technique*). The equipment is easily packed away and stored, so this technique can be utilized discreetly.

Clysmatics push a gently pressured flow of water into the colon, which is allowed to build up until a strong desire to empty the colon is created. Once emptied, the colon refills with water until another release is required. This process is repeated several times. The unique design of the clysmatic allows the inflow nozzle to remain in the anus while the bowel evacuation is taking place. This design feature protects the clean water that is waiting to enter the colon from the evacuation by use of a one-way valve. This allows the technique to be completed without the need for re-insertion.

This constant flushing of water in and out of the colon removes mucous and faeces, but the main purpose of the technique, however, is to stimulate all the reflexes within the colon. This stimulation is similar to an internal massage and has the potential to create movement and release in all parts of the body.

This technique can be very useful where consistent constipation is a problem, as it will help to clear the bowel and tone the muscles, helping to re-educate the bowel. It is also useful during a cleansing programme to help stimulate deep tissue release and in stagnant lymphatic situations (e.g. a cold, 'flu or a sore throat).

Upon completion of this technique, people can feel light-headed, in which case rest is recommended.

To apply this technique you will need:

- I clysmatic
- 5–8 litres (9–14 pints) of filtered water

Instructions

1. Set up the clysmatic, as described in the manufacturer's instructions.

2. Fill the container with 5–8 litres (9–14 pints) of water at body temperature.

3. Lubricate the anal region.

4. Sit on the nozzle.

5. Open the tap to allow water to flow through.

6. While water is entering, contract the anal sphincter, allowing the water to fill up the colon.

7. When the pressure in the colon begins to become uncomfortable, release the anal sphincter to release the bowel contents.

8. Repeat this process until the reservoir of water is emptied. You can also add any of the substances that you can add to enemas, apart from oil, to enhance the therapeutic effects of the water.

COLONICS

A colonic passes 15 litres (26 pints) of water through the colon. The speculum used enables water to flow in and waste to leave simultaneously. The water is built up to fill the entire colon by pinching the waste pipe. When the water reaches the ileocoecal valve at the far end of the colon, the colon creates an energetic flush, pushing the contents of the colon out through the waste pipe.

The first 5 litres (9 pints) of water are administered with the client lying on their left side so that the cleansing mainly takes place in the descending colon. The second and third 5 litres (9 pints) are usually administered with the client lying on their back (with their knees up), so that the water can reach the far side of the colon. This position also enables the abdomen to be massaged to facilitate a better colon cleanse.

The constant flushing of water in and out of the colon removes mucous and faeces. Like the clysmatic, however, the main purpose of this technique is to stimulate all the reflexes within the colon to create movement and release in all parts of the body.

This technique can be very useful where consistent constipation is a problem, as it will clear the bowel and tone the muscles, helping to re-educate the bowel. It can be helpful during a cleansing programme to help deep tissue release, in stagnant lymphatic situations and before and after a fast. Some people use this technique at the spring equinox to give the body a kick-start in taking full advantage of the cleansing properties of spring.

Upon completion of this technique, some people can feel tired and light-headed, and some can feel quite toxic for the following few days. To apply this technique you will need to make an appointment with a colonic therapist.

URINE THERAPY

When I talked with the local people during my travels to different parts of the world, I discovered that all of the old cultures practised urine therapy. Using urine as a healing tool dates back thousands of years. It has many different applications, from treating wounds and burns to changing the charge around the cell membrane. It is used both externally and internally, but it is the external use of urine that I have found particularly helpful in my work.

Urine is basically an overflow of the lymphatic system and is completely sterile when passed unless there is a specific urinary or kidney infection. The use of urine as a therapy is called *isopathy*, meaning 'identical treating identical', as opposed to *homoeopathy*, which is 'like treating like'. Your urine holds within it all the information of who you really are, along with a rich mixture of vitamins and minerals. It is very useful for both drawing out toxicity and cleansing.

When using urine externally, collect your first passing of the day. The old Indian urine therapists used to say of this morning collection, 'Reject the head and tail of the serpent.' This means that you collect the urine midstream. Pour it into a glass bottle and allow the air to get to it by lightly placing a cotton wool bung in the top of the bottle. Don't put it in the fridge, but store it in a cool dark place for a minimum of three days. The urine is now ideal to use externally because it has undergone a chemical change. As it is exposed to the air, it becomes more alkaline and this gives it the property of drawing inflammation out of the body. It does this by drawing sodium out of the cells and out through the skin. This makes urine rubbing the quickest way to change the charge around the cell membrane and therefore the overall body charge. Externally, urine that is 3–10 days old is used. This has both a cleansing and an anti-inflammatory effect.

Full-Body Urine Rubbing

Instructions

1. Warm up a bottle of 3–10-day-old urine by placing the bottle in a jug of warm water. Pour the warmed urine into a bowl (classically this was a copper container).

2. Sit in your bath or shower and begin by wetting your bare hands with urine and rubbing the urine into your face and neck until they are dry (i.e. until the urine has been absorbed and the skin is dry).

3. Next, rub urine into both feet, top and bottom, again until the skin is dry.

4. Work your way up your body, reaching all the parts you can, and always rubbing the urine in until the skin is dry – some areas will absorb it more quickly than others. It works on the high elimination areas well, but you can be random in your application.

5. When you have rubbed urine into your entire body (front and back), once again rub your face and neck until the skin is dry.

6. Have a shower or bath and wash with a natural soap.

7. Obviously this process can take some time. Indeed, in an ideal situation you would rub for an hour.

However, if you are short of time, try just rubbing the face, neck, soles of the feet and palms, as these are the main outlet areas of the skin.

It is very nice as part of a general maintenance programme to do a skin brush followed by a 20-minute full-body urine rub and then finish off with some hot and cold showering. This makes an excellent way to kick-start your day, especially if you have a lot to do.

Full-body urine rubbing can be done weekly or daily, depending on the intensity of the movement required. It is particularly useful for people who are unable to draw toxicity out of the body via enemas.

Urine Packing

Urine packing can have an amazing effect upon the body, and packing the kidneys is especially powerful. I have known people with nephritis who, within an hour of applying a urine pack to their kidneys, have had a dramatic reduction in their symptoms. In this situation, even packing with fresh urine (if no old urine is available) can be most helpful.

In our study of the five elements we learned that the kidneys are the seat of fear, so packing the kidneys with urine can be very helpful when people are in a state of high anxiety or fear. I have also noticed this to be particularly useful in cases of ulcerative colitis, where I can often hear the fear and anxiety in the voice of the person. In these situations I often recommend that the person initially applies a urine pack to their kidneys every evening for a minimum of an hour and continues with this practice until their level of fear and anxiety subsides.

To apply this technique you will need:

- a small piece of unbleached brushed cotton or similar cloth about the size of a tea towel
- a bottle of your own urine that is 3–10 days old
- a roll of cling film or similar material

Instructions

1. Warm the urine up by placing the bottle in a jug of warm water.

2. Pour the urine onto the cloth, making sure the whole area is wet.

3. Wring out any excess urine and apply the pack to the kidney area (the mid to lower back).

4. Cover the pack in cling film to prevent leakage.

5. Lie down and relax for an hour.

6. Remove the pack and wash or shower.

NOTE *There is no need to apply extra heat (e.g. a hot water bottle) to a urine pack.*

Urine packs can be applied to all sorts of other areas of the body with great effect. In situations where women have had the lymph nodes under their arms removed, urine packing to the underarms helps to open up a route of elimination and ease lymph blockages in this area. Another area that responds very powerfully to urine packing is the thyroid. If someone has an underactive thyroid, full body rubbing combined with packing to the thyroid can be very helpful. I find that a half-hour castor oil pack followed by a half-hour urine pack to the thyroid can bring a lot of healing energy to this area. The lungs, especially when congested, also respond very favourably to urine packing, as does any area that is swollen or inflamed.

Fresh urine can be used almost anywhere on the body. It can be used in a footbath to help draw toxicity out through the soles of the feet, for example. It is also remarkable for curing most types of earache. If a child has an earache, try placing a couple of drops of its own or its mother's fresh urine in the ears. It is wonderful for the eyes (try bathing your eyes morning and evening with fresh urine or placing a couple of drops in each eye). This is one of the best ways I have found to quickly and effectively treat conjunctivitis. When used in a nasal douche (sometimes called a neti), urine greatly helps to clear the sinuses. Fresh urine placed in the hair and left for an hour before washing (cover the head in a towel) has a great softening effect and improves the quality of the hair and scalp. Indeed, one of the chief components of urine, urea, is used in a great many commercial hair and skin products. This urea is invariably collected from the urine of animals. Surely it is much more preferable to use your own? It is quite common after someone has begun the practice of urine rubbing to find that people comment on how healthy and vital their skin looks.

Internal Urine Therapy

Drinking your own urine can have a remarkable effect on your body and mind and has been practised for thousands of years. Indeed, it is a much more common practice even today than you might at first imagine. Once again it is the morning passing, midstream, which is traditionally used.

If you want to start gently, I recommend just rinsing your mouth out with some fresh morning urine, which is also one of the most effective treatments I know for gingivitis and bleeding gums. Then you might like to try gargling with morning urine.

When it comes to actually drinking urine, I recommend that at first you start with a few sips of fresh urine taken midstream in the late afternoon, as this will be milder than the morning passing. You can then increase the amount of this urine that you drink, and once you feel comfortable, switch to drinking the first passing of the morning.

When drinking your own urine you need to be very aware of what I call the 'push and pull'. If you are drinking urine, which is your true vibration, it will create a process of detoxification as your body begins to release substances that do not hold your vibration. If you are doing this cleansing work from within, it is also important to do urine rubs so that you pull the toxicity out from the body through the skin. This is what I mean when I talk about matching the push and pull. This also makes the use of urine one of the most powerful of all the techniques. Furthermore, it is completely free and readily available anywhere because you always have urine with you.

NOTE *Taking urine internally is not recommended for those who eat much meat or take regular medication.*

All of the above techniques can be very powerful and very healing when employed at the correct time, but they do need to be used wisely. Your feelings are your best guide. Only do a technique when it feels right to do so. Techniques should not be applied randomly in the hope of bringing about change. They should be applied with a clear understanding of which specific areas need support or targeting.

Techniques are really all about helping you to connect at a deeper level with who you really are. When you give the body extra tools like these to aid its cleansing and healing process, it will reward you with a deeper connection with yourself. As you use them, your intuition will become stronger, so that you will feel when it is the right time to practise a technique and will intuitively know which technique to perform, for how long and with the exact level of intensity to suit you at that particular moment in time. Techniques can greatly ease the extra pressure placed upon the body during the healing process and are all potentially hugely consciousness altering.

Glossary

acute illness: A short-lived illness requiring lots of energy.

biochemical processes: Chemical and physio-chemical processes that occur within living organisms.

bio-photon: A photon produced in the body by the collision of two free radicals.

blood–brain barrier: A barrier, formed by specialized endothelial cells in the blood capillaries, which separates the brain from the main circulatory system and so protects the central nervous system.

cell membrane: The outer boundary of a cell, which has major control over the cell's function; it is made of lipids and protein.

chronic illness: A deep, stagnant illness that is more difficult to shift than an acute illness.

co-dependence: Where a person relies on another person in some way for their wellbeing and esteem.

colostrum: Also known as 'first milk' or 'beestings', the substance produced by a woman in late pregnancy and during the first few days after birth.

electrolytes: The macro-minerals – sodium, potassium, calcium and magnesium.

electron: A negatively charged subatomic particle, the primary carrier of electricity in solids.

enzymes: Proteins produced by a living organism to act as a catalyst for a biochemical reaction.

equinox: A time of equal day and night, when the sun is at right angles to the equator. Usually around 21 March and 21 September.

extracellular fluids: All body fluids outside the cells, referred to as the 'humours' in ancient physiological theory.

inflammation: A biological and protective response by the body intended to remove harmful stimuli and to initiate the healing process.

ion: An atom or molecule with either a positive or negative charge.

macrocosm: The bigger picture, the universe, the cosmos.

metabolism: The chemical processes that occur within a living organism to maintain life.

microbe: A micro-organism, especially a bacterium.

microcosm: An encapsulation in miniature – the small encapsulation of the bigger picture (the macrocosm).

micro-organism: A very small life form.

microzymes: Living organisms contained in healthy cells which, under certain circumstances, could evolve into bacteria to instigate changes. They could then change back when balance had been created. Imperishable and found in all forms of life (plant up to human), Béchamp considered them a basic constituent of life.

night terrors: Frightening dreams that usually occur during the first three to four hours of non-REM sleep (whereas nightmares occur during REM sleep). Characterized by extreme distress, shouting and rapid heartbeat.

nodal: A zero point. Current or voltage.

permeable: Allowing liquids or gases to pass through.

pH: A measure of acidity or alkalinity.

photon: Particle representing a quantum of light.

polarity: The distinction between positive and negative.

predisposition: The energetic blueprint inherited from earlier generations.

prostaglandins: A group of compounds with varying, hormone-like effects working with the endocrine glands.

suppressive treatment: Treatment preventing an expression by the person, which would have led to an improvement in overall health and wellbeing.

transmutation: Transformation from one substance or state into another.

Further Reading

Nancy Appleton, *The Curse of Louis Pasteur*, Choice, 1999

J. W. Armstong, *The Water of Life: A Treatise on Urine Therapy*, True Health Publishing Company, 1951; reissued Vermilion, 2005

Edward Bach, *Heal Thyself*, C.W. Daniel, 1996

Dr F. Batmanghelidj, *Your Body's Many Cries for Water*, Global Health Solutions, 1994

Harriet Beinfield, *Between Heaven and Earth*, Ballantine Books, Inc., 1992

Marco Bischof, *Biophotonen: Das Licht in unseren Zellen* (*Biophotons: The Light in our Cells*, as yet untranslated into English), Zweitausendeins, 1996

Gregg Braden, *The Divine Matrix*, Hay House, 2006

James Braley and Ron Hoggan, Dangerous Grains: *Why Gluten Cereal Grains May Be Hazardous to Your Health*, Avery Health Guides, 2003

David Brownstein MD, *Iodine: Why You Need It*, Alternative Medical Press, 2008

Lawrence Broxmeyer MD, 'Influenza and the TB connection', *Nexus* vol. 18, no. 6, October–November 2011, p.17

Martin L. Budd, *Low Blood Sugar*, Thorsons, 1981

Johanna Budwig, *Flax Oil as a True Aid Against Arthritis, Heart Infarction, Cancer and Other Diseases*, Apple Publishing Co. Ltd, 1994

Carolyn Dean, *The Miracle of Magnesium*, Random House, Inc., 2003

Jared Diamond, *The World Until Yesterday*, Allen Lane, 2012

Masaru Emoto, *The Hidden Messages in Water*, Beyond Words Publishing, 2004

Max Gerson, *A Cancer Therapy,* The Gerson Institute, 1958

Elaine Gottschall, *Breaking the Vicious Cycle: Intestinal Health Through Diet*, Kirkton Press Ltd, 1994

Graham Gynn and Tony Wright, *Left in the Dark*, Kaleidos Press, 2008

Annie Padden Jubb and David Jubb, *Secrets of an Alkaline Body*, North Atlantic Books, 2004

Robin Lim, *Placenta: The Forgotten Chakra*

Bruce Lipton, *The Biology of Belief,* Hay House, 2008

Christine Maggiore, *What If Everything You Thought You Knew About AIDS Was Wrong?*, Bridge of Love, 1996

William A. McGarey, *The Oil That Heals*, ARE Press, 1994

Lynne McTaggart, *The Field*, HarperCollins, 2001

Vladimir Megré, *Anastasia*, Ringing Cedars Press, 2005

Johanna Paunegger and Thomas Poppe, *Moontime*, C.W. Daniel Co. Ltd., 1995

Carl Pfeiffer, *Zinc and Other Micronutrients*, Keats Publishing, Inc., 1978

Weston Price, *Nutrition and Physical Degeneration*, P. B. Hoeber, 1939; reissued Price Pottenger Nutrition, 2008

Gill Rapley and Tracey Murkett, *Baby-Led Weaning*, Vermilion, 2008

Janine Roberts, *Fear of the Invisible*, Impact Investigative Media Productions, 2008

Roger Taylor, 'Free Radicals and the Wholeness of the Organism', *Nexus*, vol. 13, no. 3, April–May 2006

Peter Tompkins and Christopher Bird, *Secrets of the Soil*, Earthpulse Press, 1998

The College of Natural Nutrition DVDs

Human Potential, 2007

Working with Natural Rhythms: The Five Element Theory, 2007

How to Take a Case History, 2007

Online

Grow Your Own Babies Blog: www.growyourownbabies.co.uk/blog/

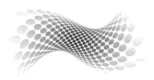

Index

JOIN THE HAY HOUSE FAMILY

As the leading self-help, mind, body and spirit publisher in the UK, we'd like to welcome you to our family so that you can enjoy all the benefits our website has to offer.

 EXTRACTS from a selection of your favourite author titles

 COMPETITIONS, PRIZES & SPECIAL OFFERS Win extracts, money off, downloads and so much more

 LISTEN to a range of radio interviews and our latest audio publications

 CELEBRATE YOUR BIRTHDAY An inspiring gift will be sent your way

 LATEST NEWS Keep up with the latest news from and about our authors

 ATTEND OUR AUTHOR EVENTS Be the first to hear about our author events

 **iPHONE APPS** Download your favourite app for your iPhone

 HAY HOUSE INFORMATION Ask us anything; all enquiries answered

join us online at **www.hayhouse.co.uk**

 Astley House, 33 Notting Hill Gate
London, W11 3JQ
T: 020 3675 2450 E: info@hayhouse.co.uk

ABOUT THE AUTHOR

Author photo: Jenni Watters

Barbara Wren has been teaching and lecturing for the past 30 years, showing people a different approach to healing through nutrition and healing techniques. She has been practising for 35 years, and has always believed that the empowerment of individuals through contacting their own inner wisdom is the only true way back to wholeness and happiness within the universal laws and rhythms.

The uniqueness of her College of Natural Nutrition approach is always at the leading edge of healing the body so that it can dance with the universal rhythms and respond positively to ongoing changes.

www.natnut.co.uk